RIVER FISHING

RIVER FISHING

Len Head

THE CROWOOD PRESS

First published in 1985 by
THE CROWOOD PRESS
Ramsbury, Marlborough
Wiltshire SN8 2HE

British Library Cataloguing in Publication Data

Head, Len
River fishing.
1. Fishing–Great Britain
I. Title
799.1'2 SH605

ISBN 0-946284-71-7

Typeset by Inforum Limited, Portsmouth
Printed in Great Britain

Contents

Len Head

Introduction

An angling acquaintance once told me that his life's ambition was to retire to a town with a river running through it. That made me realise how fortunate I was to be brought up within casting distance of the Suffolk Stour where I cut my angling teeth. Many a season has passed since my début on its banks, but I remember as if they were yesterday the trips in a leaky old boat with my father and uncles. The intervening years have seen change. Some beautiful spots on the river have disappeared for ever, victims of the dredger. But although my fishing interests have diversified into still waters, I have never lost my deep love of fishing in streams, tributaries and rivers throughout the country.

There is a world of difference between rivers and stillwaters. Having spent much time fishing both, I have no hesitation in saying that rivers generally are more interesting and more demanding of skills and techniques. They require a wider diversity and know-how along with a deeper understanding of watercraft.

There is a line of thought contending that stillwater fish are harder to tempt because they have unlimited time to inspect the bait closely, whereas river fish must make up their minds before the current sweeps the tackle downstream. I do not share that view: good presentation is vital in both spheres. Stillwater fishing mostly is about ensuring that bait behaves naturally and offers no resistance to a taking fish, and I believe those requirements are more easily achieved with only the specific gravity of the water to consider. Baits trotted along a river must be continuously and expertly controlled so that they appear natural to the fish despite the vagaries of current speed, depths and flow patterns.

There is more to think about in river fishing. The current is stronger on the surface than at the bottom, and the difference must be accounted for in your arrangement of tackle. The bait must ride over bottom debris without snagging or appearing suspicious. Tackle needs coaxing, controlling and manipulating to allow the bait to rise or fall naturally into or over irregularities in the river bed. Bait must travel through the swim at the same depth and speed as the groundbait. Good presentation of legered and static baits entails manoeuvring the tackle through or into spots where food is naturally washed by the current. If only one of the many factors is wrong or ignored, the bait will be rejected by all but tiddlers.

No two swims on a river are ever alike. Rivers differ in size, character, depth and speed according to gradient and geology. Because of the vast differences in the terrain of Britain, the angler may find himself on the banks of a big, clear gravel bottomed river, or beside a sedate, silted, coloured flatland stream. Every river itself varies in character between its upper and lower reaches. Versatility is therefore the keynote for the all-round river coarse angler who must continually change approach and tactics in order to get the best sport from the great variety offered.

Reading the water, or watercraft, is second nature to the experienced angler and is the most important skill to culti-

vate. Regrettably, watercraft is very difficult to describe and even the best writers have failed to put the message across with the clarity it deserves. However, it is always obvious whether a fisherman has the skill or not: it is an amalgam of observation, experience and sixth sense that tells the gifted angler which swims are likely to hold different species of fish, what sizes they will be, and how they should best be tackled.

In the following chapters I have tried to convey some impression of the sorts of swims to look for when you hunt particular species, but there is still no substitute for developing your own sense of watercraft; and the only way to do that is by going to the river as often as possible, and noting the structure of swims which do or do not produce fish.

Part of watercraft is knowing when to fish for which species. It is no good saying that next Saturday you will fish for bream, or whatever, then sticking to your decision regardless of conditions. They could prove hopeless for bream but perfect for another species, another stretch or even another river. Instead, watch the weather pattern and plan accordingly. Then your catches will soar.

Assuming that the reader already has some background knowledge of fishing, I have not dealt with the elements of tackle and technique. Also, the book is not about specimen hunting specifically (although I believe that becoming skilful enough to catch good numbers of fish will lead in due course to a few specimens in your net provided the river holds them), nor does it claim to be an encyclopedia of river fishing in all its aspects. You will find no reference to game fishing, to grayling, to tiddler snatching or to match fishing. Instead I have confined myself to the major river species, and the tactics described are not necessarily those that catch most fish. Rather, they are the ones I know to be enjoyable as well as successful. After all, it is enjoyment that takes us fishing in the first place.

(Opposite) River fishing flourishes despite man's intervention along the banks.

1 Chub

You can always spot a successful chub angler. He will be drably dressed, he moves slowly and approaches his swim in a low crouch. He treads softly; landing net and bag are laid quietly on the bank. He knows – and I trust that by the end of the chapter you will appreciate why – that 90 per cent of the art of chub fishing is about not scaring the fish. A frightened chub is not the least bit hungry.

It is unlikely that any other river species has senses so finely tuned to detect underwater sounds. Water is an excellent conductor of sound waves, though chub and other cyprinids do not hear in quite the way humans do. They are equipped to 'feel' sounds instead, and this they do by sensing pressure changes caused by disturbances in the water and above the surface. The commotion made by a careless angler is instantly detected and tells the chub to get out of there fast.

A lecture in fish physiology is out of context here even if I were qualified to deliver it. For the moment then, just be assured that despite its obvious lack of ears, a chub probably has the most sensitive 'hearing' system of any river fish. It has keen eyesight as well, which makes it extremely important for anglers to keep quiet and out of sight and to make use of any available cover on the bank.

Provided that stealth is accepted as being the cardinal rule of chub fishing, you will find the species to be the most obliging of the worthwhile-sized fish in the river. Rarely are conditions totally hopeless. Blazing midsummer heat waves when you feel like jumping in with the fish, midwinter days when toes turn to ice lollies, floods or drought, a chub or two is always on the cards if the swim is carefully selected.

HABITAT AND BEHAVIOUR

Most chub swims are near cover of some kind, classic examples being overhanging bankside trees and bushes, and under rafts of debris that form around trailing branches. Alder trees provide the best overhung swims of all, which no doubt explains the traditional nickname for chub, Alderman. Loggerhead is another name, and very appropriate when you look at the chub's large, blunt head. Chevin and chavender are yet more nicknames, but I do not know where they originate. In Scotland chub are known as Sckellies.

Underwater roots, fallen branches, undercut banks, rush beds (especially where they have toppled over to form an arch), weir piles, bridge supports and the shade of the bridge itself are all very attractive to chub. They will live anywhere that provides cover, security and a

(Opposite) A 4lb fish — specimen weight from most rivers.

Small chub are easily confused with dace.

bolt hole – but only if strength of current is to their liking.

Although snaggy swims are the most reliable places to find chub, they are found in some open stretches of river. Good spots are where the stream narrows and its pace quickens or where a sidestream joins and diverts the main flow. In the latter case, chub prefer to lie in the slacks and eddies between the lines of main and inflowing current. Like roach, chub are fond of a gravel bottom. The perfect swim would be a medium fast glide over clean gravel, about 4ft deep, and beneath a dense overhang. Observant chub anglers should find such spots easily enough.

Speed of current is the deciding factor. I know lots of apparently promising swims which remain chubless because the currents are wrong. It is said that chub prefer the current to run at a slow walking pace, and I agree with that. Tiny whirlpools curling along the water's surface are one indicator of suitable current speed. They often denote some minor obstruction upstream which itself is probably unimportant, but they occur so often in many of the finest chub swims that I know it cannot be mere coincidence.

Tackle

It is possible to catch chub on small hooks and frail tackle more suited to minnow bashing, and indeed some anglers prefer to fish this way. Some even land a few of the chub they hook. Many more are lost because the tackle breaks. To my mind this amounts to bad angling – how often have you heard a light tackle addict bemoaning his lost fish!

Surely no responsible fisherman wants his quarry to trail broken end tackle. It is much better to come properly equipped with tackle strong enough to land chub reasonably quickly. In any case, most of the excitement of real chub hunting is lost messing about with tiddler gear. Proper chubbing is all about the thrill of a bucking rod in the confines of a snaggy swim. Your tackle must be strong enough to ensure that the fish comes out.

Using a 10 or 11ft through action 1lb test curve Avon-type rod, fixed spool reel loaded with 5lb line, plus a few spare spools holding lines between 4 and 8lb, a chub fisherman is properly equipped to deal with any legering situation. Once my standard rod was 10ft long and incorporated a quiver tip that made it ideal for legering. Trouble was, I frequently came across swims that were better float-fished, and of course the leger rod was hopeless for the job. These days I neglect quiver tips, good as they are, in favour of a more versatile 11ft Avon with which I can leger or float fish as the swim demands.

Stalking summer chub in a Stour backwater.

TACTICS AND TECHNIQUES

Summer Chub

Summer chub are the easiest to catch because their high metabolic rate means they are nearly always ready to have a go at a bait. They are relatively easy to locate if you look into the water through polarising glasses. The most exciting sport is had in overgrown backwaters and upper reaches, the more remote the better. It is surprising how many miles of meandering upper reaches, tributaries and backwaters are virtually untrodden by anglers. Superb sport is available if you explore.

A typical small river has lots of chubby characteristics. Many have not been 'improved' by the dredger, therefore much of the bottom will be gravel. Weed growth is natural and luxuriant, and the banksides are well grown with overhanging vegetation – a chub fisher's Mecca. Shallow gravelly runs with a reasonably smooth flow provide the most reliable summer hotspots. For some reason chub sometimes seem to lose much of their innate caution in shallow water and can be suckers for any well-placed bait. Part of the explanation is that where several fish occupy the same swim, competition for titbits is fierce. I think also that water running over gravel is quite noisy for chub and diffuses unnatural sounds like footsteps and rod rests being skewered into hard ground. There is less chance of the chub becoming aware of the angler's presence.

If you walk along the banks of a clear stream and peer into the water through Polaroids, you are almost sure to spot the unmistakable shapes of chub. They have distinctive blackish tails, pinky-orange pectoral and ventral fins and thick, rubbery lips. They lurk near rush beds or drift slowly in and out of patches of shade.

Paul Norris specialises in freelined slug baits.

Simplicity of tackle is the keynote for chubbing on small rivers. You must be mobile and explore every likely looking swim. This you cannot do loaded down with huge tackle boxes and rod bags. The basic equipment is rod, reel, landing net, hooks size 10 – 4, a box of swan shot, a couple of Avon floats, optional weighing scales and bait of course. I am usually happy with a loaf of fresh bread, but chub are notorious for the enormous variety of baits they will accept. Summer chub engulf anything edible that is presented naturally – assuming they have not been alarmed. Curiously enough, naturally can mean the bait hitting the water with a sploosh. Chub are accustomed to food dropping heavily into the river, and will often rush in and grab a bait before you have chance to close the bale arm.

Baits

Unusual baits may catch chub that have refused normal offerings. I have had my share on strange baits ranging from french fries and eel cutlets to dead mice. Flake, crust, slugs, lobworms and crayfish are my favourites in that order. Crayfish probably would head the list but in the rivers I fish they have declined so drastically that I hesitate to sacrifice the few that remain, particularly when I am able to catch chub easily on more plentiful baits. Brook lampreys are a stupendous chub bait though even scarcer than crays. Stone loach are good baits, more plentiful and easily caught by carefully looking under stones in the shallows or by parting the strands of silkweed which grows on weir sills. With care they can be scooped up with your bare hands.

Most small bait-sized fish (live or dead) catch chub. They work far better in summer than winter. I have experimented with fish baits in winter, believing they might sort out the better quality chub, but the results have always been disappointing. Friends tell me they use them effectively right through the cold months so it must be a question of fishing with them to find out if your particular chub respond.

Upstream Techniques

Most summer chub anglers tend to fish by casting the bait downstream, but in so doing they increase the risk of being spotted by chub that lie head to current – that is, facing you. Better sport results from approaching the fish from behind, by casting upstream and keeping out of sight. The baits I have mentioned are weighty enough to cast alone, so no lead is required on the line. An exception is when baiting with sunken crust, which needs a large shot pinched on the line 2–3in above the hook.

The killing method is to flick a bait upstream to plop into the run in which you have spotted chub or where you suspect they may lie. The unweighted bait begins to sink slowly and travels back towards you in the current. Usually it does not travel far before a chub grabs it. In really clear water you can watch the bait drifting down and see the chub move to intercept it. Exciting fishing!

I hate slugs – horrible, slimy creatures – but they are perfect for upstream fishing. Chub go crazy for them. Paul 'Slugger' Norris, the best slug angler I know, invariably gives me a good trouncing whenever we fish together. A trip to the Suffolk Stour was a classic example. Paul arrived clutching a gallon container brimming with slugs – big brown ones kept moist and lively in shredded, damp newspaper. (Slugs must be fresh and lively to catch chub.)

Part of Paul's success is his willingness to explore the impenetrable overgrown swims where others fear to tread. His first choice of swim lay beyond a jungle of head-high, vicious stinging-nettles; an unfished, chubby little run of water beside a midstream bed of bulrushes. Like roach, chub love to be around bulrushes. I watched Paul attach a size 4 hook on a 6lb line to a slug's saddle. Slugs provide a solid, compact weight for pinpoint long casting, so a flick of Paul's rod sent the bait some 15yd upstream to plop into the head of the run. We saw the semi-buoyant slug drift back towards us, sinking very slowly while Paul recovered the slack line and took great care not to disturb the bait's natural flow. We saw the flash of bronze, the swirl and an eruption of water as the hook bit home. It is fatal to show chub the slightest mercy in these tight swims. Use adequate tackle, screw the reel's clutch down tight, and haul. That's what Paul did, and his first chub was in the net inside a minute.

When you cannot see chub take the bait – any bait – bites are detected by watching the line where it enters the water. Several patterns emerge, depending on how the chub reacts. The most common is when the line jerks sideways then either falls slack as the chub turns towards you or snakes upstream if the fish runs that way. Strike a slack liner as soon as you see the bite; a chub moving in the other direction will probably pull the rod tip down before you can hit it.

Some chub just open their mouths, suck the bait in and lie there. The line slowly tightens as if the bait has snagged in weeds. On a few occasions the chub takes the bait then just drifts back with the current. This is rather difficult to detect because all you see is a slight twitch of the line. The rule is if in doubt, hit it.

The disturbance of hauling one chub from a tight swim usually ensures that no more will be tempted from the spot until they get over the shock. That is a good

Overgrown summer chub swim.

Even a small fish will snatch a big slug.

reason for adopting the mobile approach; you can easily up stakes and move to the next swim, catch another chub, move on again, and so on. Later on, it is even worth trying the first swim again.

Paul finished his session with nine chub to 3lb 14oz on slugs, while I managed six to 3lb 9oz, four on flake and the other two on crayfish which I had stored in the freezer from way back. Live crays are killed with a tap behind the head then hooked once through the second from last segment of the tail with the hook passing into the bottom and out through the top. Instead of letting the current do the work, twitch the crayfish back along the bottom with small jerks of the rod tip, thus imitating the movements of live crays which swim backwards by flapping their tails.

Floating Crust Fishing

Stalking chub in small, clear streams is river fishing at its finest. But what about the more open, featureless stretches where the fish cannot always be seen? A good way to locate chub in these surroundings is to break up a crusty loaf and throw a couple of dozen pieces of bread into the river then follow them downstream. If chub are about, it will not be long before they begin to swirl up to the crusts and slurp them down. Here is the obvious place to start fishing.

Use floating crust bait on a size 6 hook. A 1½in square of crust is about right, and should be hooked through the crumb side then back through the crust. The line must float, so dress it with floatant to within 18in of the hook, this last piece being allowed to sink because chub often are suspicious of line floating alongside the bait. If necessary, make the nylon sink by rubbing it with putty made by mixing fuller's earth with glycerine or washing up liquid.

Cast the crust then pay off more line so that it floats downstream. Mostly there is no mistaking a bite – the crust is engulfed amid a great swirl. Sometimes, though, a chub sips down a crust as gingerly as a trout may take a fly, and the only indication of a bite is that suddenly you cannot see the bait any more. A quick strike misses fish in both circumstances. Wait for the chub to turn, then hit it.

Chub take some time to recover from spawning and may not be in good condition in summer. Retaining them in keepnets is bad news for chub – and for other fish as well for that matter – because it can only retard their recovery from the battering they inflict upon themselves. If fish must be kept, a modified carp sack is far superior to a traditional keepnet. Fish cannot rub off their protective mucus against the soft woven nylon.

Winter Chub

Winter chubbing is just as enjoyable as summer fishing though sport is slower after late autumn. As compensation, chub are in superb fighting condition having fully recovered from spawning. Many summer haunts like the pockets and runs between rush beds are gone; others, like overhangs and snaggy swims, fish well all year if the current maintains a comfortable speed. When the current is too strong due to the increased winter flow rate it pays to search areas of slower moving water close by the summer swim. Chub usually move no further than the nearest patch of water that runs to their liking.

Sit and wait tactics catch plenty of chub, but the mobile approach of summer works as well if you adopt slightly different tactics. I like to hedge my bets by using both approaches in the one session. I begin by walking the stretch armed with a bucket of stale mashed bread or a supply of whatever other bait I intend to use. Plain mashed bread is a superb river bait, and I have had encouraging results by pepping it up with flavoured essences added to the water. Crab flavour has proven to be a winner, with honeycomb a close runner. Add about 15ml of essence to a bucket of water before mashing the bread.

I toss a handful of bait into every likely spot to interest the resident chub, then I start fishing in the first baited patch and move to each prepared swim in turn. I save what I judge to be the best swim until late evening, and there I use sit and wait tac-

1½–2lb fish are fine sport on light tackle.

tics. Overhangs and flood rafts are by far the top winter swims, and most of them are best fished by casting downstream with a fixed paternoster leger rig. The bait is presented semi-static under the overhang. Using just enough lead to hold bottom, cast downstream and level with a near-bank swim. The current will wash the tackle under the overhang so that it comes to rest in the chub's front parlour. Sometimes it is necessary to tease bait into position by lifting the rod tip so that the lead bumps further round in the current. For a far-bank swim add more lead and cast as close as possible to the edge of snags. And as I will explain later, there is another trick you can use.

I catch winter chub on smelly baits like cheese, luncheon meat and sweetcorn. Different rivers respond to different baits, and I have fished those where crust, flake or lobworms are the best baits of all. Experiment with your local chub to see which they prefer. Whatever it turns out to be, the bait still has to be worked into position.

Having got the bait settled under the overhang, keep it on the move by giving the line a half turn on the reel, or by lifting the rod point so that the tackle bumps a little farther under the swim. Chub often grab a bait they have ignored so far if you give it a sharp tug along the bottom. The usual bite indication is a nudge on the quiver or rod tip as the chub picks up the bait, followed by a powerful pull around as it turns downstream. With a belly in the line as outlined in the roach chapter, the tip springs straight before it is pulled down. Should the chub move sideways with the bait, as they often do, the lead is pulled along and causes the tip to bounce back and forth. At other times the rod slams round with no preliminaries as the chub belts off downstream. All are positive takes and easy to connect with.

In some places you may do better by exploring the water with a rolling leger bumped across the stream to search the whole river bed. Try adding a float, or cast upstream with a light lead so that the current trundles the bait back towards you. There is no doubt that chub like a moving bait in all but severe weather.

A Deadly Technique

Earlier I mentioned a method of placing a bait under the branches of a far-bank overhang. In fact I devised it to fish neatly in most of those apparently impossible swims that chub anglers come across – at the end of a long tunnel of overhanging bushes or anywhere else that restricts casting. Like many other chub anglers I used to mess around with rafts of some kind that carried the bait downstream to the inaccessible spots. The idea never worked properly because bait inevitably fell off before it reached its destination. Then there is the matter of getting the bait on to the raft in the first place.

I use a half slice of cut loaf to ferry the bait. The hook is nicked into a crusty corner and the bait – cheese, flake or whatever – is moulded around the shank. This rather ridiculous looking arrangement is lobbed into the river, whereupon the slice of bread carries its passenger to where the chub lie. En route the slice can be steered by manoeuvring the rod tip and adjusting line tension. You can send it past, into or alongside any gap or obstruction. By the time it reaches its target the bread is saturated, so a flick of the rod is all it takes to free the baited hook, which sinks in precisely the right spot.

Virtually any swim becomes a viable proposition with this method, including far bank overhangs. The whole slice can be cast with ease across a not too wide river. A bonus is that because the bait falls so

naturally to the bottom chub are more confident; indeed, immediate bites are commonplace. A variation is to attach a small surface popping plug instead of the bait, send that downstream, then work it back with small jerks on the rod tip. The plug pops and splutters as it muddles along the surface. Bites on surface plugs are electric. Water explodes under the branches and the rod slams round.

One restriction of the ferrying technique is that if you need lead on the line, it must be fixed so that it stays suspended under the floating slice. A running leger would slide down the line until it hit bottom, anchored itself and ruined the system.

Small stream chubbing in winter. The fish grabbed a bait drifted under the exposed tree roots.

Trotting

On a mild winter's day without too much wind, trotting becomes one of the most effective methods of catching chub. A trotting rod should be 12–13ft long and of slowish action, bending progressively down to the handle. 3–4lb line is the ideal match and quite strong enough to fish safely in the more open glides of river, which just happen to be the best trotting swims anyway. Step up the line where snags are present, and accept the inevitable drop in tackle control.

An Avon balsa float carrying 4–5 AA shot suits most swims. The faster the flow or the stronger the wind, the bigger it must be. While working on this chapter I fished the Norfolk Wensum when water and weather were perfect for trotting, the river carrying a little colour, a good flow and no wind. I set up my tackle on the inside and just downstream of a right angle bend where the current hit my bank then flowed diagonally across, smoothing into a perfectly paced chub run along the far bank. The rod was a 13ft carbon trotter, the reel my much prized Allcock's Popular centre pin. The Avon float carried 5 AA shot bunched together with a No.1 shot nipped on 10in above the hook, a sharpened size 8 tied direct with its barb nipped in to protect the chubs' lips and to make unhooking so much easier.

I have never found a better bait than a pinch of flake for trotting, nor a finer groundbait than soaked and flavoured stale bread that disperses in a milky cloud as it sinks. Regular handfuls thrown in draw chub from well downstream. I spent the first ten minutes feeding with ground-

(Opposite) Floating crust downstream into an obstructed swim.

bait, estimating that it would reach bottom 10yd downstream where I expected the chub would be lying. I thought I would catch a chub second trot down, but I was wrong – I got one first time. Like all winter fish hooked in a brisk stream on a responsive rod, the chub put up a spirited fight, boring strongly in the current before rolling into the net. The scales nudged down to 4lb – a good start.

Unless a chub succumbs quietly the rest of the shoal probably take alarm, so it is better to give them the benefit of the doubt by resting the swim for a few minutes, although you should still continue with periodic groundbaiting. A few trots later, down went the float and the rod again bent double into a hard fighting club, this time a shade smaller at 3lb 3oz. Chub bites on the trot are fairly characteristic. The float pauses, moves slightly sideways without submerging – or bobs violently – then goes under. Sometimes the float just sinks as if it were fouled on weeds. And indeed that is often the case, but it pays to strike all the same.

Bites slowed as the morning passed; the shoal grew more and more cagey as their numbers reduced. Subtle changes in bait presentation, plus regular feeding, kept the rod well bent until thirteen chub lay in my keep sacks. The smallest weighed 2lb 8oz, the best a beauty pulling 4lb 13oz.

Small changes in tackle often make all the difference. Moving the bottom shot up the line has the effect of increasing bait buoyancy so that it runs through the swim higher in the water. Moving the float up the line so that the bottom shot drags the river bed will slow the bait's progress. Bringing one of the big shot down to drag bottom slows it down even more. Periodically halt the float's downstream run by stopping the flow of line. This makes the bait flutter up enticingly from the bottom, then sink again as the reel is released. Odd fish tend to drop further downstream behind the main shoal, so the occasional longer trot of 40 or 50 yd might pay off. Do ring the changes, because as I said at the beginning chub are an obliging fish. But not all the chub oblige all the time; the quiet, versatile approach is the hallmark of a chub fisherman who enjoys consistently high results.

(Opposite) Chub can be lifted by the shoulders if you don't have a landing net handy.

2 Perch

I am not one of the multitude whose boyhood initiation into the world of fishing came about with the proud capture of a small, greedy perch. But it was perch which showed me that fish do not spend all day, everyday, swimming about and eating. Nor do they live in every swim along the river. I discovered that, like people, fish have dislikes and preferences as to where they live, what they do, and when and how they feed.

HABITAT AND BEHAVIOUR

I recall a big willow tree whose bole leaned precariously low over a crystal clear, gravel bottomed, steady run at the tail end of a small mill pool. A group of perch lived there, all but one being smallish fish from 6in long to perhaps half a pound. Even allowing for a youngster's vivid imagination, the biggest perch would have weighed about 1¼lb. I would straddle the bole and inch my way along the trunk until I could peer into the run and learn something of their behaviour. The fact that they were there whenever I looked and were always reluctant to leave the swim even when alarmed taught me that perch are territorial and that they like a gravel river bed. I noticed that a second willow farther down the mill tail concealed no perch despite its gravel bed. The current there was slightly more turbulent than the evenly paced run of my willow, so perch have a definite preference for certain types of flow, it seemed.

I learned that much of the time they remain hidden, lurking tight under the bank in the tree's shadow. They ventured out now and again in twos and threes to make short explorations of the swim, then vanished into the shadows again. I spent hours watching them react to items which they discovered in the swim and to disturbances such as a pebble or twig dropped into the water. The perch normally drifted with their spiny dorsal fins folded except when they made a tight turn, at which the fin rose, presumably to help with the manoeuvre. Upon coming across something interesting or edible, and in response to disturbances, they 'presented arms', fins abristle, and looking for all the world like a squad of soldiers – medium sized corporals, little privates and that big sergeant major, all ready to do battle.

The most fascinating aspect of the peepshow was watching their reactions to baits. A free worm dropped beside the shadow resulted in several perch, and sometimes all of them (though rarely the sergeant major), hurrying out, all guns blazing. Mostly, a lively worm would be swallowed by the perch quickest off the mark; but sometimes they were more hesitant, nipping at the end of the worm, shaking it and letting go. A dead worm invariably was tweaked and worried before either a perch swallowed it or rejected it altogether. Sometimes the worm lay on the river bed for ages, having been inspected and rejected by a dozen fish. Any worm tethered by hook, line and float greatly increased the likelihood of this tweaking routine and caused the bobs and dips of the

An excellent bag of winter fish on livebait for Len Head and Barry Waldron.

A perch hole.

float known to any angler.

The sergeant major was different. He remained in the shadows most of the time, seemingly content to allow his troops to snaffle the bait. Once he emerged, grabbed the head of a worm dangling from the mouth of a smaller perch and looked as though he would have swallowed both of them had the private not let go. In the end I caught most of the privates, and the corporals as well, yet the big fish always eluded me. Now, thirty-five years later the willow still leans over that mill pool but coloured water prevents me from peering into the swim.

The Perch Disease

I like to think that the perch also are there. Sadly that is a pipedream. The early 1960s saw the beginnings of the infamous perch disease which eventually spread through much of the country to decimate the species. It was not a sudden affair with hundreds of perch floating belly up. Had it been, there would have been an immediate outcry. As it was, perch simply disappeared gradually and only a few were discovered dead or in distress. The full impact went almost unnoticed until it dawned on dismayed fishermen that they no longer caught any perch except the rare survivor.

Even now, twenty years on, the cause of the disease has yet to be fully explained. I find that incredibly hard to believe: it is not unreasonable to suppose that the threat of a disease virulent enough to wipe out a valued species would spur those paid to look after anglers' interests to mount an immediate investigation. Yet it is only recently that scientists have suggested that the cause may be bacterial: an aeromonas group bacteria, common in our waters and normally harmless to fish, somehow become pathogenic. Nobody really knows what triggers an outbreak like this, or what factors predispose perch to its ravages.

The last few years have shown a heartening increase in perch numbers, and we hope this indicates a come-back. If bacteria are the cause, it is a sobering thought that the perch's return may not be permanent. Indeed, perhaps the disease still is rampant, and the apparent revival is due to a progressive immunity inbred into the new population. Let us hope so.

It is too soon to say whether perch are re-established in all or even most waters. They are prolific breeders and already are showing fairly widespread in good numbers. Not all are tiddlers: the come-back is mature enough to produce good sized fish as well. A few fish escaped the disease, and with little competition from their own kind (or from anglers who thought all the perch were gone) have managed to grow into sergeants and even majors. Big perch offer a challenge to anyone willing to look.

A vaned float rig is useful for drifting baits into distant swims.

Location

Like pike, perch generally live in easily recognised places; like weir and mill pools, deeper holes, pilings, below bridges and overhanging trees and especially below the sill of smaller pools, undercut banks, bends and corners of the river; anywhere which offers shadow is likely to hold them.

Those prominent bars on a perch's flanks are there for good reason. They transform the perch from the brightly coloured fish we see in the net to near invisibility against a background of rushes and water lily stems; and therein lies the clue to some of the very best perch swims. Although deeper water is favoured elsewhere, rush bed and lily swims need not be more than a few feet. Perch love to lurk just inside the fringes of the stems, hidden but still able to observe all that goes on outside. I once kept a small perch in an aquarium, where it spent most of its time with its face to the glass, peering out from between plastic weed stems. It soon came out when anything edible dropped into the tank.

Large numbers of very young perch shoal together and are easily caught one after another, all alike as peas in a pod. Other than that, they are not a true shoal fish in my opinion. As they grow, they divide into smaller groups that relocate in suitable holts along the river, perhaps already occupied by fish from previous generations. Thus, groups of perch often comprise a wide range of fish which have chosen to live in the same spot. You may catch a 4oz perch from one cast, and one four times heavier the next.

A good perch swim with nice depth, plenty of shadow and steady flow may contain a large head. My best river catch amounted to twenty-nine perch weighing between a few ounces and nearly 2lb, all from an 8ft deep swim on an outside bend where old sunken wooden piles lined the bank. You are unlikely to catch tiddler perch in spots that hold bigger fish – mainly because tiddlers are not fond of being eaten!

The generals of the perch world have always been enigmatic. Three and four pounders are uncommon to say the least, and perch topping 5lb are as rare as a £3 note. I believe that big fish are solitary or swim with one or two more of comparable weight. They are seldom caught because of their uncanny caution and a lack of pressure from specialist anglers. The big ones are as hard to catch as small perch are easy, and would call for a single-minded and dedicated approach. Perch have been known to live for twenty-five years, and no fish lives that long without learning something about avoiding fishermen.

Lively lobworms usually guarantee brisk sport.

Baits

Stillwater perch are often seen rounding up a shoal of prey fish, herding them into bays and margins so shallow that the little ones even ground themselves trying to escape. While I have seen this happen on upper reaches of a river I have not come across it lower down. Strangely enough I have never found perch particularly easy to catch during those frenzies, though a tiny spinner or deadbait drawn through the swim may take odd fish.

Very young perch feed on insect larvae, shrimps and such, then soon switch to small fish. Bigger perch still feed on the smaller aquatic creatures but are naturally more predatory on small fish of most species including their own. I have never caught perch on eel or stickleback though. Unlike pike which possess explosive acceleration for lunging at food, perch have no such thrust or speed. A glance at its slender tail wrist, caudal fin and generally humpbacked profile shows clearly that a perch is not built for acceleration. It is, however, a superb acrobat which utilises its ability to chase and outswim a selected victim amongst a shoal of food fish. It twists, turns, snaps at its victim's tail and shadows its every movement until the little fish is sufficiently damaged or exhausted to be swallowed.

On most rivers small live fish account for most decent sized perch. Stone loach were a favourite of mine when I could find them, followed by a little perch about 3–4in long. Minnows and gudgeons are almost as good, though roach, dace and other species will all be taken. Lobworms catch perch, and sometimes outfish live baits. For some reason I have done better with worms on the small, clear-water upper reaches of rivers but I cannot explain why they should work better there than farther downriver. In general worms are not quite as selective as fish baits as regards the size of perch hooked. The smallest perch will tackle a worm twice its size.

Lobworm tail properly presented.

It is important that worms are lively. Reflecting on those perch under the willow bole, I remember that a limp, bedraggled, dead worm dangling from the hook is unlikely to score. I keep my worms active by storing them in a spacious container filled with screwed up, damp newspaper together with a few tufts of moss, turning the container upside down occasionally so that the worms work their way to the bottom and back.

You may find that on cold winter days smaller breeds of worms are accepted while lobs and livebaits are refused. Red worms and marsh worms are the best in my experience because they wriggle even in

Optonic heads and butt ring indicator arrangement.

freezing water. I have little faith in brandlings for perch or anything else, though I cannot deny that they have accounted for a good many perch.

Spinning

Spinning is rather overrated, I think, and I have never enjoyed it. Perhaps my lack of enthusiasm explains my comparative lack of success. I am a firm believer that an angler rarely will become good at any aspect of fishing that he does not enjoy. That said, spinning is an uncluttered, easy way of catching perch, with no need to lug big tackle boxes, rod bags and livebait buckets along the river bank. All you need is rod and reel, a net, a few lures and unhooking instruments.

Perch are easily spooked by continually pulling a lure through their patch especially when one or two of them have been caught, pricked or lost. Therefore I recommend keeping on the move. Mostly you are unlikely to hook more than one or two perch from each swim, however many it holds. Perch are aggressive and great chasers of lures, but often refuse to take, especially in a swim that has already produced a couple of fish. They still snatch and nip at the lure as it is retrieved – you can feel them through the rod tip. The lure may be pursued right into the bank, and you will see the flash of the perch's flanks as it turns away. Changing the lure, its size, colour, action and speed of retrieve may tempt a few more takes but if the perch persist in merely following you are better off moving to the next swim. You can always return later.

Having said that spinning is overrated, nevertheless I rate it highly as a perch *finder* and use it whenever I fish a strange river where I have not been able to prelocate likely swims. I work a lure through any likely looking area until either a fish follows the lure to the bank and I spot it, or I feel one tapping away as I retrieve. Either way I then settle down to fish the swim with conventional tackle and baits, the approach I prefer.

Tiny revolving bar spoons seem more attractive than wobbling lures. I have never found anything better than the well-known Mepps bar spoon for a deep retrieve, and even the smallest are heavy enough to cast well with no added lead, which I think spoils a lure's action. Other

(Opposite) Now recovering from Aeromonas disease, river perch are making a strong come back.

models worth trying are Ondex, Voblex, Veltic and Vibros. Striped patterns seem particularly effective, and small Devon minnows also will score. Although worms can be deadly when fished sink-and-draw, paradoxically lures work better with a slow, steady, straight recovery.

The lure's colouration is also important as a perch attractor. For hundreds of years perch anglers have realised the effectiveness of incorporating something within the red end of the spectrum. If the lure itself lacks the necessary colour, add a tuft of bright red or orange wool or feather just above the rear treble hook. Scientists say that a perch sees little or no blue but does recognise green almost as well as red, so this highlights a useful area for lure experimentation. We are told that perch also have a degree of infra-red vision, though I am not sure how we could capitalise on that.

TACTICS AND TECHNIQUES

So, perch have excellent vision, feed by sight, and probably very little by smell. (Even so, I always nip the tips off worms anyway to release their scent, and I think I get better results by so doing.) The knowledge that they feed predominantly by sight explains why a lively bait fished sink-and-draw or tweaked along the bottom is nearly always more rewarding than a static offering. The exceptions are those off days, usually in mid-winter, when a tethered but still lively bait is more attractive to the odd fish. In those conditions they are in no mood for a chase, so it is necessary to place the bait accurately into their holt.

I do not want to give the impression that perch do not feed well in winter. As a matter of fact November through to the end of the season sees the cream of river perch fishing. Mild spells are the times to concentrate upon, when water temperatures are somewhere between the mid-40s and low-50s Fahrenheit. A mild March is a wonderful time to be out after perch, for those final precious days of the season usually mean perfect temperatures and hot feeding spells. Dirty, coloured water or flood conditions put a damper on sport however favourable the temperatures may be. Even though they live in murky shadows, perch are less sensitive to light levels than are other species. Given the choice, choose an overcast day to fish, but never let brightness deter you from making a trip to the river. Provided you know where perch are and can place a bait into their dim parlours, there is every chance of good sport.

Handle perch with care. Hold them gently, and use forceps or a disgorger to remove the hook.

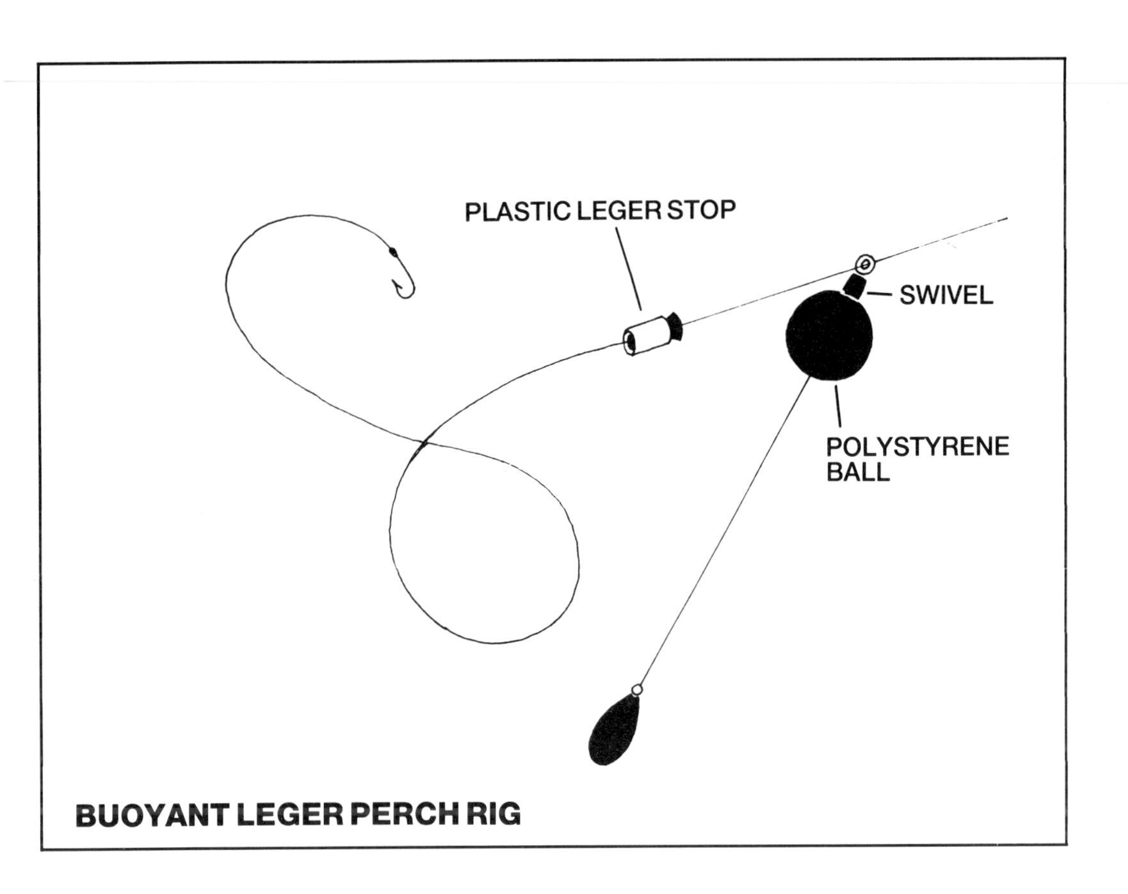

BUOYANT LEGER PERCH RIG

Tackle

Perch do not grow to enormous sizes and, although a hooked fish fights quite hard, by no stretch of the imagination can it be described as powerful. I cannot recall having to give line to a perch even on very light tackle. That being so, they are one of the few species that have never inspired a special rod design. For legering, a 10–11ft compound tapered rod of light Avon action will be just about perfect; it doubles for spinning as well if, like me, you dislike those short rods sold for the purpose. Look no further than a 12–13ft medium-power match rod for general float fishing. Choose rods with a softish action because perch have a thin membrane at the sides of the mouth just behind the lips. When the hook takes hold there you need a soft, responsive action to avoid pulling it out. Soft rods are more fun to catch perch on anyway.

Line strengths and hook sizes should be matched to the method, bait, swim and size of perch expected. I do most of my fishing with 3lb line, and carry spare spools of 4, 5 and 6lb for varying situations and snaggy swims. Size 8 or 6 hooks are suited to big lobworms hooked once about a third down from the head. Sizes 6 and 4 are for livebaits hooked through the lips. You do not need tandem hooks or trebles for perch fishing.

As a rule of thumb, tackle up as lightly as you dare, bearing in mind the swim's restrictions. I know that little perch readily commit suicide on the coarsest of tackle, but better fish are tackle shy and will leave the bait upon feeling the slightest hint of resistance. It pays to put a lot of care into your terminal tackle arrangement so that a biting fish is able to take line freely. A leger rig should be free-running with the hook tail long enough to eliminate friction. My perch rigs always incorporate buoyancy which keeps the swivel holding the reel line well clear of the bottom and thus ensures it does not clog with debris. The buoyant rig further permits a legered livebait extra swimming range so that it is more likely to be spotted by a hungry stripy.

Bite Indication

Quiver and swing tips are out of place for legering because perch play with the bait for some time before taking it. You need a method that allows the fish plenty of resistance-free line. Most perch swims are in slow or steady flows where it is possible to use an indicator hung below the butt ring or between butt and second. With its weight nicely counterbalanced to the strength of the flow, the indicator imposes no resistance. The time-honoured dough bobbin suffices, as does a tube of tin foil. However, I prefer my own ring or clip indicator which is used without modification on most of my river legering rods. If the ring is too light to counteract the current, add some lead wire ballast. A characteristic perch bite sets the indicator rising towards the rod in fits and starts. Let the ring hang well below the rod so that the bite has time to develop more positively. If necessary open the bale arm and feed extra line to the fish. Bites on small baits can safely be struck quickly. Exactly when to strike takes on large baits like lobworms and livebaits is often a matter of hit and miss.

I worry about deep-hooking perch: they may seem to swim off happily when released but I have seen a number turn belly up soon afterwards. Logic tells me to strike sooner to avoid deep-hooking, yet doing so guarantees missing a high proportion of bites and in any case an immediate strike often results in a throat-hooked perch anyway. Delayed striking loses few fish but risks damaging the fish; even so, a good number are lip hooked by this technique. Working out the right tactics on the day and striking according to the bites produced does not solve the problem either. The first fish may take a yard of line and be hooked in the lip; the next is throat-hooked even if you give just a couple of inches of line. Stalemate! Hedge your bets by striking when the indicator climbs more deliberately. More important, get into the rigid habit of using hooks with the barbs nipped in. At least they are easily extracted and give a perch the benefit of having the odds of survival more in its favour.

Worms and livebaits are effectively legered on the bottom, particularly when given a periodic tweak by jerking the line near the reel. Both baits can be deadly fished off the bottom, either by trotting them through the swim with the float set to present them about a foot above the river bed or anchored with a running paternoster float rig, using as small a float and as little lead as necessary. Bites on the latter rig are usually positive and may be struck after a short pause.

Freelined, slow sinking lobworm is the most productive method I know, and although not selective in the size of perch caught it has accounted for my best ever

(Opposite) Perch and its victim.

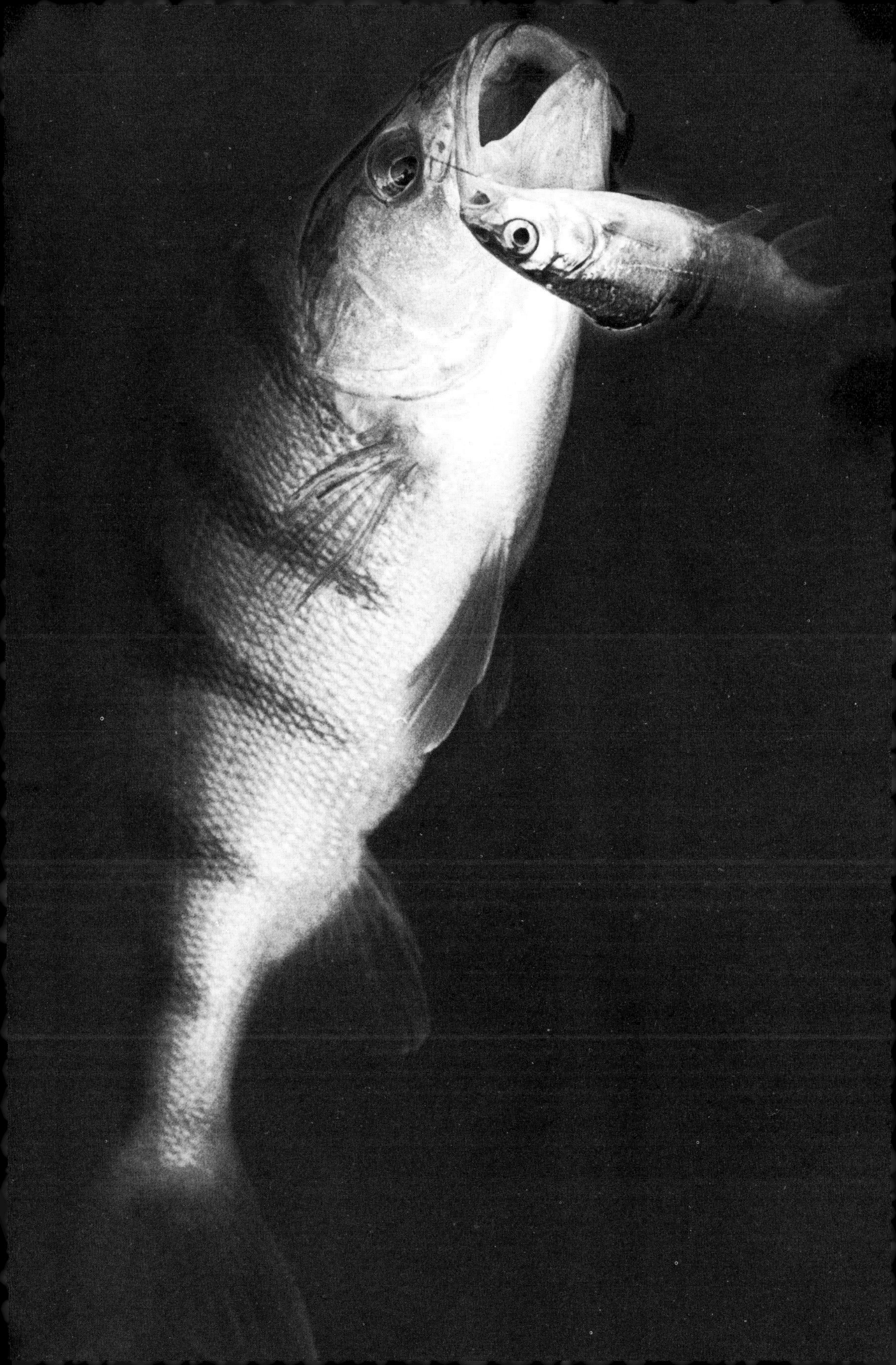

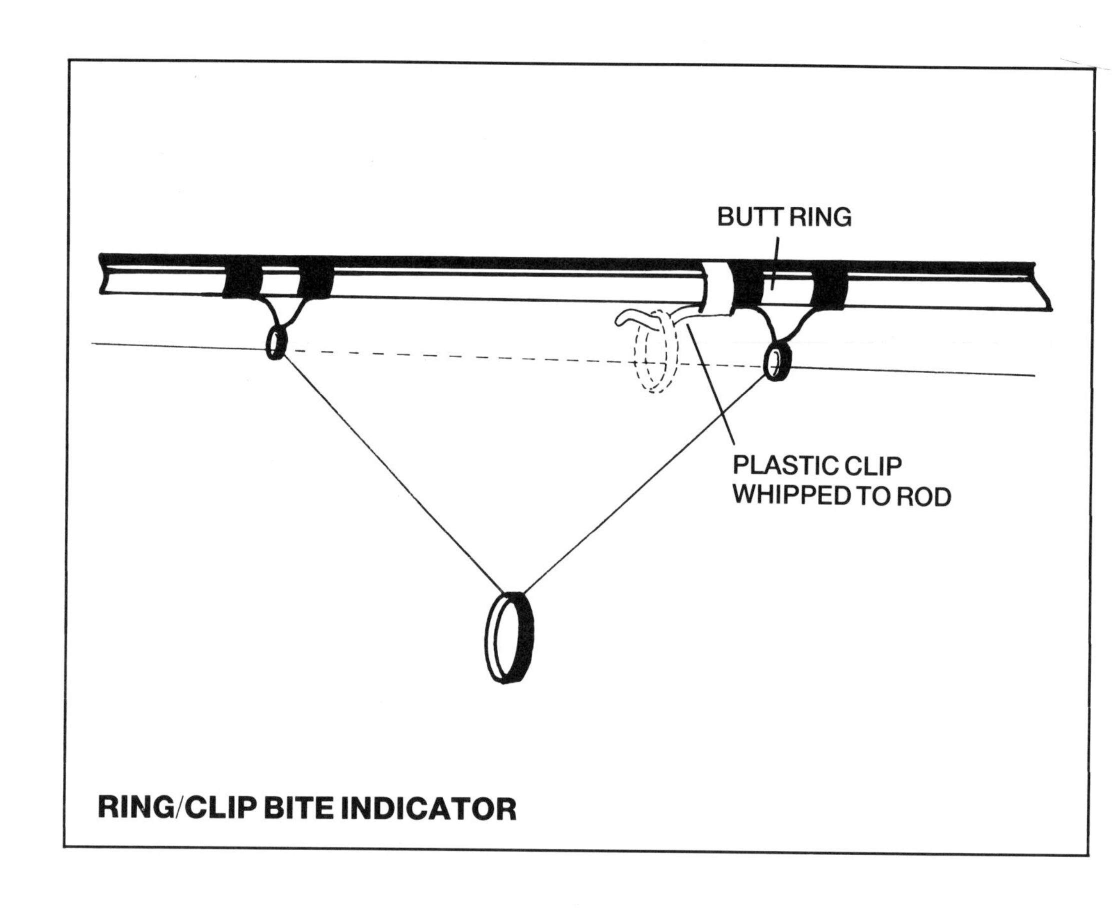

RING/CLIP BITE INDICATOR

fish of just over 3lb. A variation equally deadly is to add a self-cocking float, with no lead on the line, set so that the sinking worm finally is suspended just above the bottom. Let it trot through the swim.

Perch hiding in the fringes of a rush-bed swim call for pinpoint casting to the very edge of the rush stems. In these surroundings perch are reluctant to leave hiding to intercept your bait. You could leger, but I am not happy with that because a taking fish may swim back into the rushes and the bite indicator is unable to register which way it is running. A float is the answer. A sliding float fixed bottom end only allows an attractive fall to the bait and aids accurate casting. Nip a single shot big enough to cock the float to the line about 9in above the hook. Next tie a stop knot far enough above the float to suspend the bait or to allow the laying-on technique. On normal fixed float tackle, even cast accurately, the bait sinks in an arc away from the rushes and finishes up well away from the hotspot. A slider provides a compact rig that not only casts well but also allows the bait to sink tight up to the rushes as line is drawn through the float eye. Bottom end only floats are also a lot less likely to snag if a hooked fish runs into cover.

As in zander fishing, a choice must be made between using a wire trace and catching fewer perch, or using monofil or Dacron at risk of leaving hooks in some of the pike almost certain to attack the livebaits. There is no doubt that a heavy wire trace results in dropped baits, so until the tackle makers come up with a light, extra supple wire of about 4lb test, I compromise by opting for a short length of 15–20lb Dacron.

Retaining the Catch

It is known that a scared or injured fish can release 'fear substances' into the water, and that when a fish raises the alarm that smell or sense is transmitted to the rest of the shoal which react with fright or increased caution. Perhaps perch have this ability particularly well developed, for I am sure that returning one immediately to the swim nearly always spells the end of sport for some time. For that reason I make an exception to my general rule of quickly returning my fish, preferring to keep perch until the end of the session. However, do not put them into a loose carp sack. I learned the hard way that the loose folds of nylon cling around the gills and prevent breathing. Carp sacks held open by supporting rings are ideal though, and thus modified are far superior to keepnets which enmesh the perch's sharp spines and gill covers.

3 Barbel

It is unfortunate that barbel are found in only a few British rivers, best known being the Hampshire Avon, Dorset Stour, Kennet, Thames, Severn, Swale and Ure. The Hertfordshire Lee still holds respectable numbers, and Norfolk's Wensum is increasingly viable since its recent stocking with a hundred fish. The once prolific Trent shows heartening signs of a come back, and I suspect it will again become a premier barbel water in years to come.

Barbel are something of an enigma among river fish, at times so easy to catch, at others nigh impossible. The latter is more common by far. Early season fishing in June and July are the most productive times, then the fish become progressively slower throughout summer. They are quick to learn, and soon you must work very hard for every fish you catch. Late September and October see a revival of more consistent fishing especially for big fish, and October is arguably the best month of all for real heavyweights.

With the first period of pronounced frosts comes the end of consistent sport. From then on, throughout winter, barbel can still be caught when weather and water conditions are right; for example during mild westerly and southerly winds that bring enough rain to raise the river level and increase its colour and flow.

My barbel career was late to start, mainly because there is no river containing them within easy reach. I still live far away, but since taking that first trip to the Hampshire Avon some ten years ago I am well and truly hooked on those powerful, whiskered torpedoes. I make the pilgrimage to barbel country as often as I can.

Barbel Spotting

The first visit was an eye-opener. Peering into the crystal water of the Avon from high on a suspension bridge, I was convinced that the river must be devoid of any fish, let alone barbel. Billowing masses of ranunculus fronds waved in the fast flow and revealed glimpses of clean gravel that appeared and disappeared in tune with the swaying weed and currents. As I watched and my eyes adjusted, life began to materialise beneath the surface. Three dark shapes nosed from the shadow of the bridge. Dark backs and black tails identified them as chub. Two brilliantly coloured perch hung in a small patch of quiet water behind a bridge support and occasionally drifted across to a slack by the near bank to send a shoal of minnows darting for cover.

Of barbel there was no sign until Paul softly called me across to the other side of the bridge. 'Barbel,' he said. 'Good ones too, on the gravel bar there.' He pointed into the river. I scanned the water and squinted; but I could see no barbel. 'Right against the edge of the weed,' said Paul who is an old hand at spotting them. 'Can't you see their big pectoral fins?' Squinting still harder, sure enough I picked out the pink triangles of fin, then the indistinct shape of the fish themselves with their slightly asymmetrical tails. Barbel spotting is an art most anglers need time to cultivate before they become proficient. Unless the light is particularly good it is easily possible to stare at a bare patch of gravel for ages before a movement catches your eye and you realise that a barbel was lying there all the time.

With experience you learn to pick out the fins or spot the dark tail poking out from behind fronds of weed. The top lobe is longer and pointed, the bottom shorter and rounded. Consistent sport with barbel depends on locating them beforehand, so it is well worth spending some time cultivating the art. Obviously one cannot always spot fish. Sometimes they are hidden in deep or distant runs, or the water is too coloured. With practice though a swim pattern begins to build up in your mind, and although you cannot see the fish you can relate the speed and set of current in a strange swim to the patterns of a known barbel swim. An educated guess may drop a bait in the right area.

HABITAT AND BEHAVIOUR

Much of the time you will be wrong, but then I do not know any barbel angler who is right all the time. Barbel lying motionless under weeds are probably not feeding, but may well be tempted out by judicious groundbaiting. Feeding fish are much easier to spot because they periodically drift from weeds to gravel to intercept food coming down with the current. Sometimes you see a flash of bronze as the barbel turns sideways on. I am not sure why they flash. Some fishermen claim that the underslung mouth makes it difficult to grab passing suspended food, and the turn of the body makes feeding an easier business. I doubt that this is the reason because I have seen flashing fish that I am sure were not feeding. The flash sometimes follows the fish scraping its flanks along the gravel as though freeing itself from parasites.

Whatever the explanation, flashing is a welcome sight for any barbel hunter. Whether they are feeding or not, at least he has located his fish. Occasionally, especially towards evening or in coloured water, barbel also roll on the surface. Actually, it is more of a slicing action or head-and-tailing rather like bream. Where you see barbel working is obviously the right place to fish. If you cannot spot them, look for other clues instead. Barbel are synonymous with weeds and are rarely far away from them, but that is hardly a clue for the barbel beginner. In my early days I recall asking the bailiff who issued my day ticket where I might find barbel, having explained that I had not fished the river before. He replied bluntly, 'Anywhere there is weed.' A fat lot of help that was, since the river was solid with it from bank to bank.

Location

The most productive high summer swims are often found in the shallower, weedier, fast stretches where by carefully watching the movements of weed fronds you can see the clear gravel runs beneath. Even the smallest patch may be worth fishing, though larger areas are definitely a better bet. Barbel feed by sucking in and blowing out bottom debris including the gravel. Any gravel patch regularly visited by the species develops a cleaner, yellower appearance than its surroundings. Most of the really productive barbel spots are quite distinctive and clean. Depressions in the river bed are none too easily found but are worth searching for. It does not have to be significantly deeper – just a few extra inches of water provides a real hotspot. Depressions are formed by the scouring, sweeping action of a dense bed of trailing weed that is pushed by the current. One such spot springs to mind: only inches

deeper than the main river bed and just a couple of yards long, it has yielded remarkable catches of barbel to just under 10lb.

Find such a swim and chances are you will catch barbel there. The fish probably like depressions because food naturally is deposited there by the currents. For the same reasons, obstructions on the river bed like boulders, stumps and bridge supports are worth a look. Barbel lie immediately downstream and behind them.

Deep, powerful runs, fast water on the edge of slacks, overhangs, undercuts and bankside runs beside marginal rushes are well worth exploring provided there is gravel and weed. Weirpools are notoriously difficult to fish because continual variations of current make accurate fishing in any chosen spot somewhat hit and miss. No two casts are likely to end up in the same spot and it is impossible to know precisely where the groundbait lies on the bottom. For all that, weirpools nearly always will contain barbel especially early in the season. Big swimfeeders cast to the edges of the fast water and into the side eddies and weir tail will take fish, as will light leger tackle cast into the white water and allowed to be towed under the weir sill by the bank eddies, or trundled around searching the bottom contours.

Tackle

Fast taper rods are out of place for barbel. Choose a nice bendy 11ft Avon of 1–1¼lb test curve and optional spliced or detachable quiver tip for legering in most swims. In overgrown or really snaggy water a light carp rod lends a better margin of safety. Trotting rods need a similar easy but not sloppy action. Stiffer blanks fail to cushion the jarring fight of a hooked barbel. Most swims and conditions can be handled by a fixed spool reel with a range of spools holding 4–8lb line, and you will find that even 10lb line is not too strong for the snaggy spots.

Barbel are notorious hook benders, so strong forged patterns are required especially when small sizes are used. There are plenty of strong hooks available in sizes bigger than 10; below that the choice is limited – Au Lion d'Or 1534, Mustad 7780C, Gold Strike and VMC 9284 are the best I know.

Every year sees more barbel caught on swimfeeder leger tackle than on all other methods put together. This is no surprise, for a feeder is a very positive way to get a concentrated trickle of feed into the swim. You can be sure that it lies close to the hookbait as well. Block end and open feeders are effective but you may need to enlarge the holes in block ends to improve the flow rate. The feed must go into the swim, not scatter all over the river when you retrieve the tackle. Use a block end for neat maggots and an open ender plugged with groundbait for inert bait like casters, corn and hemp.

TACTICS AND TECHNIQUES

Baits and Groundbaits

Hemp is a superb barbel attractor. You have only to feed hemp into a barbel swim to realise what a powerful attractor it is. If there are any fish in the area, it will not be long before their whiskery faces peer out of the weed to detect the source of the grains.

(Opposite) Even medium-weight fish are a real prize for today's barbel enthusiast.

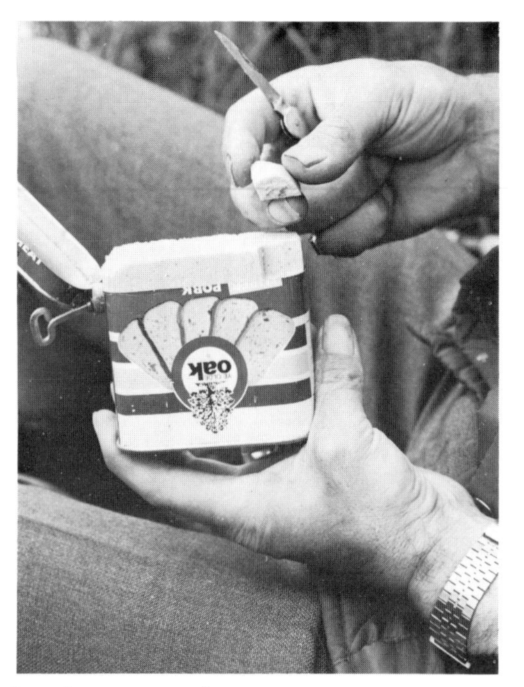

Luncheon meat cubes.

The bailiff of a well-known barbel beat told me that next to location the best way to be sure that fish are in the swim and feeding is to 'get the dining table well laid.' In other words, put in a lot of groundbait. He reckoned that it did not matter too much what went into the water as long as it was edible. Quantity is what counts.

My experience confirms this is often the case, especially early in the season. I have even used home-made swimfeeders the size of dustbins to deliver the goods. But beware: barbel in hard-flogged stretches can bolt from such heavy bombardment. I also question that any old bait will do, and I prefer to introduce good quality groundbait and hookbait samples.

Maggots catch many barbel and are convenient and effective as groundbait because they can be fed into the swim easily and accurately with block ends or bait droppers. Luncheon meat is superb – either a large chunk on a good sized hook or a smaller cube with similar free offerings in a feeder or dropper. Introduce free offerings of larger cubes by tying a length of PVA string on to the lead link, then threading on six or seven pieces of meat with a baiting needle. Tie a knot around the last one. Bait the hook with the same sized cube, and cast in. The PVA melts and the feed trickles down beside the hookbait.

Other traditional baits like sausage meat, cheese, corn and lobworms still catch plenty of barbel, and opportunities for experimenting with many more baits are there for the taking. Regular baiting with mass particle baits like maple, gunga or chick peas, tares and black eyed beans

Flavoured sweetcorn can be a killer.

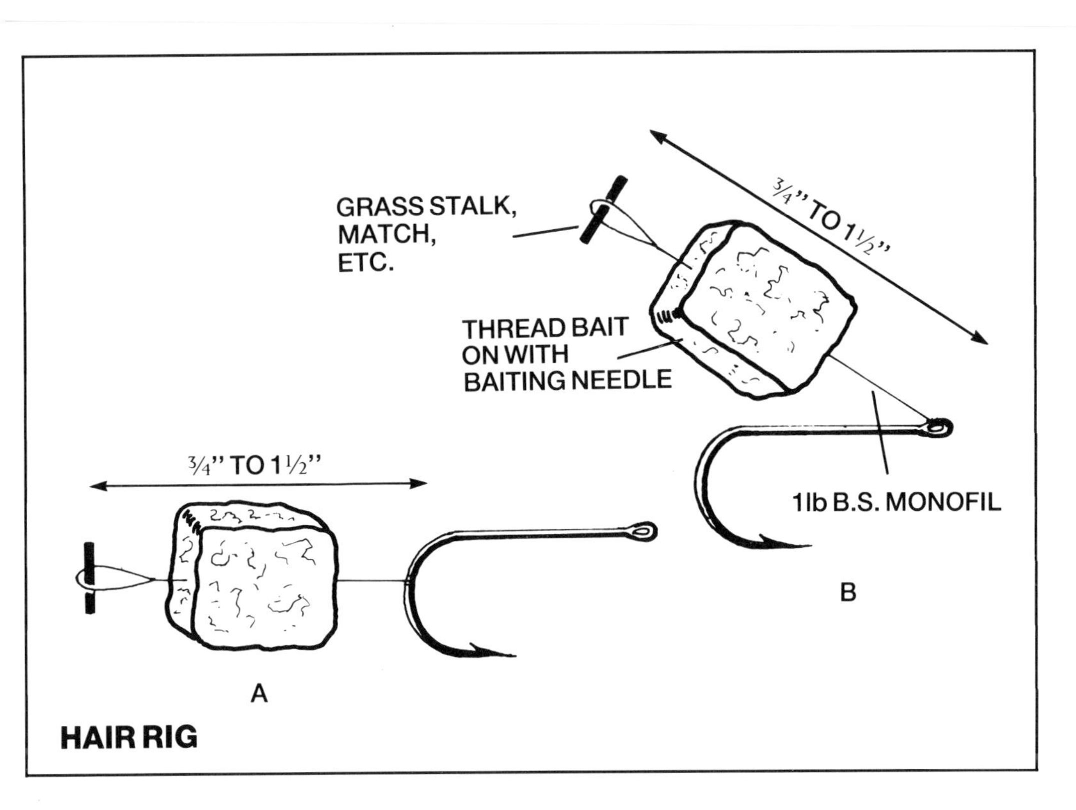

HAIR RIG

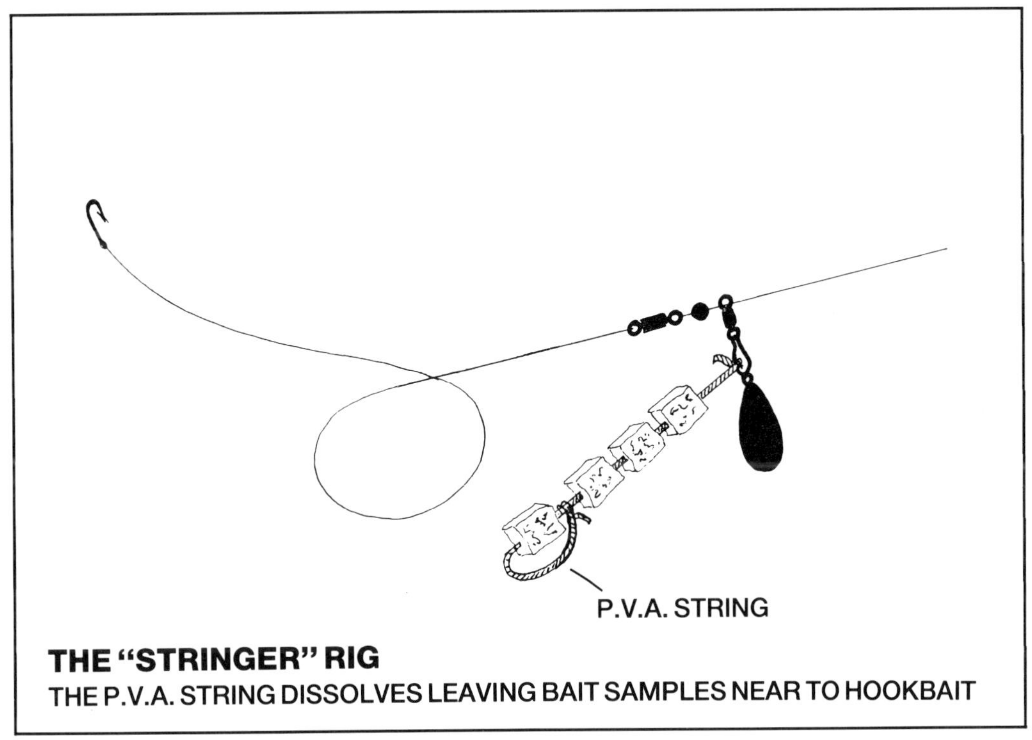

THE "STRINGER" RIG

THE P.V.A. STRING DISSOLVES LEAVING BAIT SAMPLES NEAR TO HOOKBAIT

would ensure a new lease of life for many hard-fished reaches especially if flavours and/or dyes were added, of that I'm sure. I have used flavoured, red sweetcorn with success.

Baits are flavoured by soaking in water containing about 10ml of essence to 4pts. It is a mistake to overdo it since too much flavour may repel instead of attract. Add dye to the water as well. The following day, simmer the bait for about 20min. I usually boil bait in the water and dye it has been soaked in – but only when my wife Joan is out. If it boils over, you end up with a Technicolor cooker. Similar comments apply to carp specials and protein-based baits. I am sure that an angler working with a bucket of mini-boilies and a swim full of barbel would be in for a red letter day if he had already weaned the fish on to them with a prebaiting programme.

Legering

Searching the swim with a rolling leger is a killing method at times, and is very useful when you are uncertain where the barbel lie. Obviously, when a swim is solid with weed the idea does not work; but where patches are not so dense it is possible to trundle the bait into potential holding spots until you pinpoint the barbel. Use enough lead so that the tackle holds, but will lift and bump cross-stream when the rod tip is raised. Work systematically, gradually lengthening the cast across and down river until the whole swim has been covered. If you get a bite, the spot can be fished with a static feeder, or you can continue with the rolling lead. Experiment will show which is better on the day – remember that the barbel call the tune.

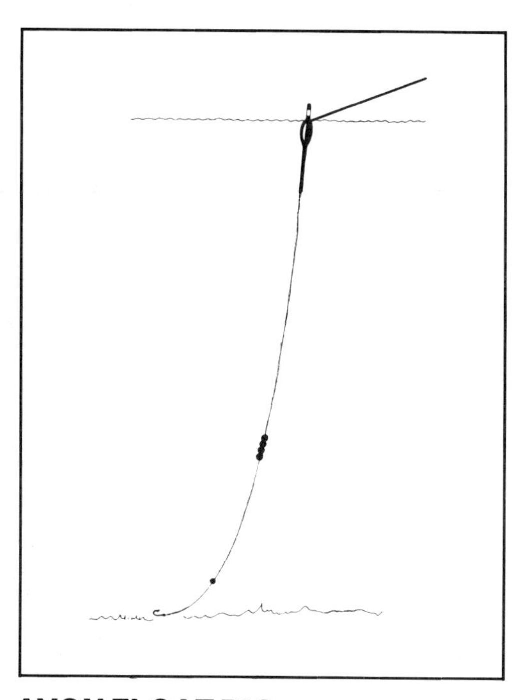

AVON FLOAT RIG FOR FAST FLOWS

A swan shot leger link suits the method because it is easy to add shot to match the current. Keep the link short though. I think that long ones allow the bait to flutter too high in the water. Occasional barbel are hooked a little above the river bed, but the majority are taken hard down on the bottom.

Upstream legering is an excellent technique in itself, and is even more useful in awkward swims that cannot be fished very well by casting downstream. Again, use just enough lead to hold bottom (and you may be surprised how little that is) with a semi-tight line and the rod propped high in its rest to minimise the length of line in the

(Opposite) Barbel love fast water and dense weeds.

water. This way there is less chance of the current catching the line and dragging your tackle out of position. Bites register by the tip pulling straight and the line falling slack. A long, sweeping strike is necessary to pick up the slack and set the hook.

Beginners may have trouble casting accurately with cumbersome feeder tackle. Often it is necessary to drop every cast with pinpoint accuracy between the waving fronds so that the feed concentrates in one place. The secret is not to try to cast straight into a gap. Instead, overcast so that the feeder lands beyond the gap. The instant before the tackle hits the river, stop the line by dropping your finger on to the spool so that the line is tight from the rod tip. Hold the rod high so that the feeder does not sink, and draw it into the gap. Then release the feeder in exactly the right position by sharply lowering the rod tip.

Trotting

Trotting is hard work but enjoyable. It is effective as well, for barbel often respond better to baits moving through the run. This method comes into its own on longer, smooth flowing runs and glides with an

Barbel fight like the devil.

A six pounder from the Lea.

even bottom and medium depth. It is very good where the swim is flanked by overhangs, rushes and other vegetation. The rod described for chub trotting is right for barbel as well. Near bank swims are best tackled with a centre pin reel; a fixed spool is preferred despite its limitations for mid-river and far bank fishing. 5lb line provides reasonable tackle control in most swims, but 4lb is even better where the weed allows. Anything less is asking for trouble unless you have a lot of experience in handling these bionic fish.

Big Avon floats are necessary for barbel trotting, with shot set on the line as shown. Most fish are taken with a bait tripping bottom, a tactic which unfortunately can result in foul hooking when the passing hook catches on the barbel's enormous outspread pectoral fin. As with trotting for any river species, it pays to ring the changes. If no bites come, try setting the float deeper and adjust the bottom shot so that the bait just drags bottom. Let the shot itself drag bottom if you like, which will slow down the trot. Holding back by feathering the line as it leaves the reel also slows the tackle; but remember that holding back too hard causes the bait to flutter from the bottom. Sometimes you need to compensate for that tendency by deepening the float setting and moving the shot closer to the hook.

Meanwhile, a steady trickle of loose feed through the swim keeps the barbel interested. A handful every cast is not too much, carefully judged to reach bottom where you expect the fish to lie. Often they will move to intercept bait hitting bottom some distance away, so extreme accuracy may not always be critical.

Playing and Netting

Hooking a fish on relatively light trotting tackle calls for extra care. The harder you bully a barbel, the harder it bullies you back – so the answer for trotting gear is to take it easy. Gentle playing provokes none of the nerve jangling jolts and rushes you get when really bending into a fish on heavier tackle. Then, a barbel feels not unlike a turbo-charged bag of nuts and bolts. Leger tackle usually triggers explosive runs because the combination of terminal lead, current on the line and rod pressure results in the fish hooking itself as it moves off with the bait. This also explains why most barbel bites wrench the rod tip over: the fish is hooked and into its first run by the time you get the rod into action.

First try to get downstream of the barbel so that you are pulling it down through the weeds rather than upstream or across. You do not get many fish into the net by trying to haul them upstream through dense weeds – a fish beds down in the weed and no amount of pulling will free it. It is a good idea to place your landing net a suitable distance down river where it will lay ready when you have played the barbel to the bank.

Even experts are broken sometimes when trotting with lighter tackle. In any case, the fight on such frail gear involves such a long duel that the poor old barbel, which habitually fights to the last, is finally netted totally exhausted and too weak to swim away when returned. Most barbel need nursing anyway. Hold the fish with its head to the current until it regains strength. Do not let it go until it is able to

(Opposite) Summer barbel fishing.

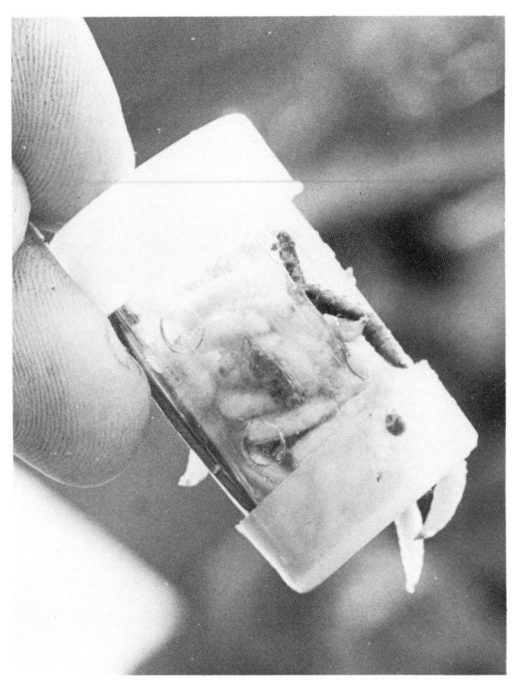

Loaded feeder.

look after itself. Sometimes you may be fooled into believing the fish is ready to go, but it waddles into the current, turns belly up and floats away. There is grave danger that the barbel will die because it cannot breathe, so before you release your grip, be sure that beautiful fish has fully revived.

An Outing for Spooky Barbel

Such bold bites may fool the newcomer into thinking that catching barbel is easy. They can be on the right day in the right swim, but sometimes they prove more cussed than the canniest chub. I discovered that one trip to the Hampshire Avon and Dorset Stour. Both rivers were low, clear and stale after a long, dry summer. The barbel had been heavily fished – that was patently obvious by their suspicion of every conventional bait offered. Finding fish in the low river was a simple matter of walking the banks and looking into the water through Polaroids. Either they were out on clean gravel or revealed glimpses of pink fin and forked tail as they lay partly hidden under weeds. Now and again I found a swim that screamed barbel although none could be seen.

I have said that extra clean gravel patches may well be feeding places, so if I came across such a swim I would watch patiently for a visiting fish. Any gravel patch with a slightly sloping bed – no matter which way it slopes – may also be worth waiting and watching, as are the depressions I mentioned (provided there is weed adjacent).

When poor light prevents fish spotting, it becomes a matter of choosing a location, then feeding it heavily and regularly until a bite confirms your choice or until lack of them proves your theory wrong. Two hours in a blind swim makes me restless to move, but there is no denying that many a fine catch has come towards the end of a long biteless spell. Sometimes it pays to sit it out.

On this particular trip I found the barbel so easily spooked that the splash of a lead, feeder or bait dropper sent them rushing for cover. Eventually I resorted to lacing the swim with a bait dropper, placing the baited tackle into position, then waiting for the wary barbel to return after the disturbance died down. They inevitably will do that, especially if hemp is the attractor. Barbel feeding on hemp is a sight to savour. They filter into the baited zone, often materialising from apparently nowhere. One moment the gravel is bare, next you are aware of pale shapes ghosting over the feed.

You can always tell when barbel are feeding. They tilt slightly, almost imperceptibly, head down and drift systematically about the swim with underslung mouths grazing the gravel like animated vacuum cleaners. I soon found that the fish refused all normal baits and terminal set-ups. This happens because either they are suspicious of the hookbait which is heavier than free samples and therefore does not behave naturally, or they are afraid of the bait itself, having been caught or hooked on it before.

I solved the problem and finished the trip with a respectable tally by flavouring my sweetcorn bait with butterscotch, using 48in hook tails, and mounting the bait on a hair rig. The latter dodge was devised by carp anglers and is now used more and more effectively for other species as well. The diagrams are self-explanatory. On the right hair rig, bait behaves perfectly naturally and is taken without suspicion; the hook follows the bait into the barbel's mouth. Rig B turned out to be most effective, judging by the ratio of bites to hooked fish, because the bait lies almost on top of the bare hook ensuring all is sucked in.

4 Roach

Every weekend of the season, on river systems all over the country, thousands of fishermen set out their stalls for roach – the bread and butter fish of river angling. Roach are probably the most widespread of all river species, which explains their huge popularity, but there is more to it than numbers. Small to medium size fish – say up to 10oz – are such obliging biters that a competent angler can expect a netful if conditions are reasonable. At the same time the successful roach addict needs considerable skill in watercraft; he must be versatile enough to handle different rivers, swims, and weather conditions, along with the tactics, baits and tackle each demands. Occasionally decent bags are caught on stout tackle, but fine gear is normally the name of the game. Many anglers rate the skill and satisfaction of handling such delicate equipment as a prime reason for their fascination with the species.

HABITAT AND BEHAVIOUR

For all their abundance roach can at times be one of the most difficult of river fishes, refusing to feed however much skill is applied. Although tiddler roach are an exception, the better quality fish are strongly affected by light intensity and do not begin to feed until the light falls below a certain level. How do you know what that is? A long time ago Richard Walker and Fred J. Taylor used a photographic exposure meter to discover that critical point. Interesting as that may be, I do not expect anglers to worry about taking light readings before they fish. In more practical terms, the right level occurs when the sun falls below a certain angle – when it dips below the trees an hour or so before dusk. Feeding may continue for several hours after dark, then recommences during early morning until the sun rises above the critical angle.

Fortunately we see plenty of cloudy days when light is subdued enough for all-day feeding. We also encounter coloured water after heavy rain, and if conditions are right not only do roach feed all day, they provide spectacular sport besides. Shady, tree-lined swims can be worth fishing in bright conditions. In fact, overhangs may well be the only areas worth fishing when the sun shines strongly. Mists over the river reduce the light level, but they normally occur after a sudden drop in water temperature. In summer that may spur roach to feed; in winter it puts them right off.

Water Temperature

Water temperature is more important in winter than in summer. The summer fisherman who confines his activities to early and late in the day is assured of good sport for temperatures are reasonably consistent then, not falling below the point at which roach stop feeding and rarely rising

(Opposite) An autumn swim.

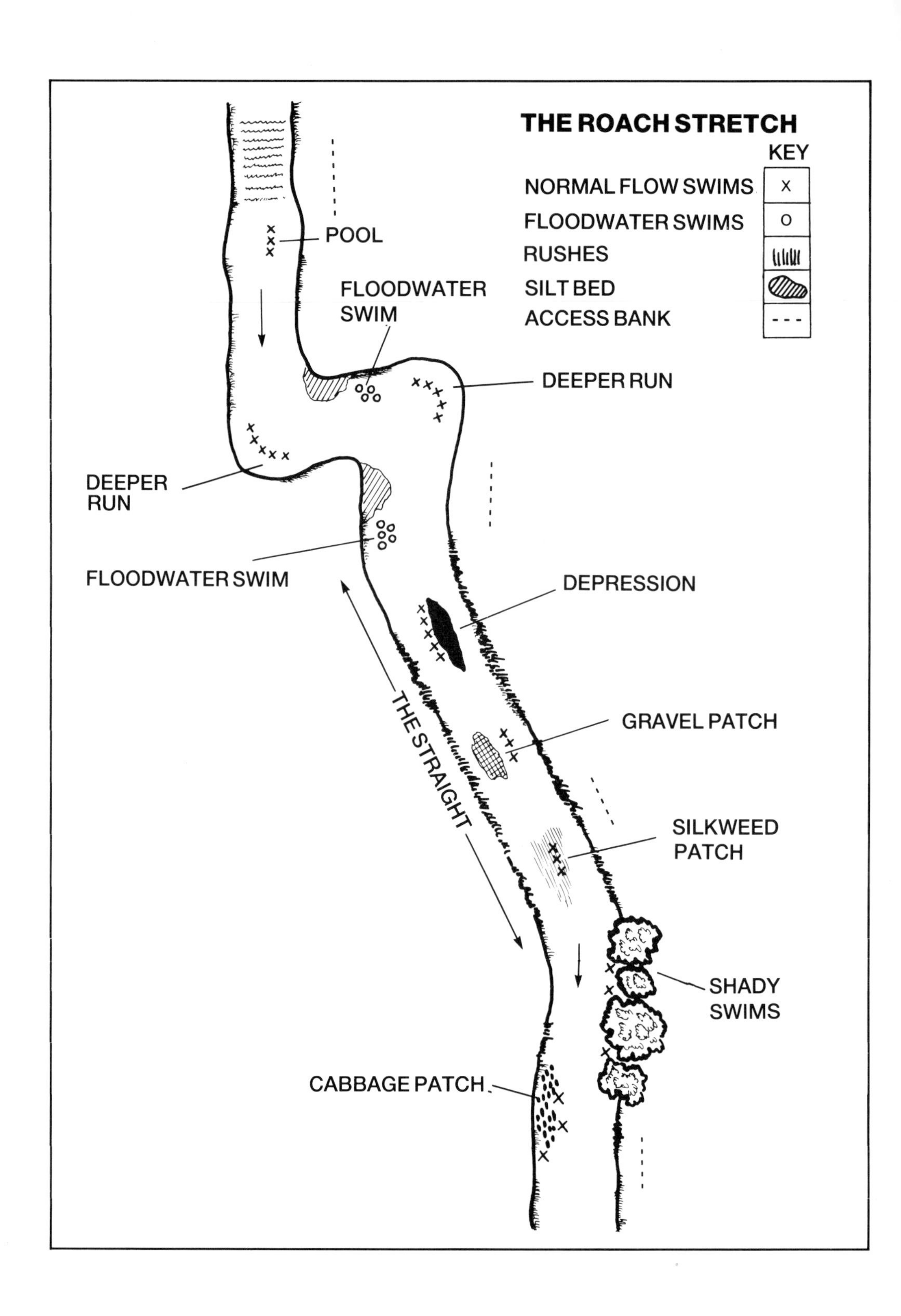
THE ROACH STRETCH
KEY
NORMAL FLOW SWIMS
FLOODWATER SWIMS
RUSHES
SILT BED
ACCESS BANK
POOL
FLOODWATER SWIM
DEEPER RUN
DEEPER RUN
FLOODWATER SWIM
DEPRESSION
THE STRAIGHT
GRAVEL PATCH
SILKWEED PATCH
SHADY SWIMS
CABBAGE PATCH

high enough to put them right off. In winter, temperature is vital. Generally, the higher it is the better; the lower it falls the less chance of a fish. At 42 degrees Fahrenheit or under you are better off fishing for something else. Fortunately, winter river temperatures are more often above 42 degrees, and in any case the most critical factor is whether it is rising, falling or steady.

A rising thermometer boosts my confidence; steady readings are good even in cold conditions; but when it is falling, even from relatively high temperatures, roach are unlikely to feed for long. Given the choice of a day when the water falls sharply from 48 degrees or when it rises a few points above 41 degrees, the latter would be my preference every time.

A big fish hooked on feeder tackle.

TACTICS AND TECHNIQUES

You often hear an experienced river fisherman refer to a particular swim or stretch as 'roachy' – something that must bewilder the less knowledgeable man. A year ago I found myself on a totally new stretch of river in which I suspected lived good shoals of decent roach. All I had to do was find them. The stretch turned out to be particularly interesting, since I discovered a whole variety of roachy spots, many of them requiring different tackle and methods. This is typical of many rivers, so follow me downstream while I point out the swims and suggest how to fish them.

The first 50yd is shallow, rippling, fast water running between bare banks and over an irregular gravelly bed. Dace are here in plenty, or they were. Those mini bow waves scurrying in all directions downstream are caused by the shoal scattering in alarm because of our clumsy approach. Chub will often lie here as well. The stretch does not look really roachy, but I point it out because there have been a few times when I accidentally hooked good roach whilst chubbing after dark on warm nights.

Quiver Tip Legering

Just below the shallows, where the river widens, deepens and the current smooths its way into the pool, live a shoal of sizeable roach. They much prefer the gentler, consistent flow over reasonable depth, which in this case slopes from the shallows into 4½ft of water, then quickly rises again at the tail of the pool. The swim does not suit trotting, my preferred method, because the pool is too small and the depth is too uneven to allow a reasonable length of trot. A longer run of even depth is best for trotting any species.

The favourite method is legering with a light action rod of about 12oz test curve and fitted with detachable or spliced in quiver tip. The rod is matched to 2½lb line and a slightly lower breaking strain hook length. I find the paternoster end rig most sensitive, used with a 48in hook tail. Heavy groundbaiting would soon spook the roach lying in the confines of this pool, so I loose feed sparingly with maggots, casters or pinches of fluffy breadflake. Many anglers have trouble connecting with roach bites whilst legering at close range, the reason being the short length of tight line from rod tip to lead. This is remedied by making longer casts from farther upstream, and by pulling off a couple of feet more line from the reel after the lead has settled. A bow of line thus lies between rod tip and lead. A quiver tip will bend slightly with the current's pull, and bites register by the tip springing partially straight then bending again as the roach turns with the bait. Short range and tight lines result in indecisive rattles of the quiver tip which are indeed difficult to hit.

Upstream legering into the pool produces better bite indication especially

Delicate jaws show the need for small baits and fine tackle.

Trotting the deep runs and holes pays off in icy conditions.

when the roach are finicky. Hook length and lead link are shortened, the lead being just heavy enough to hold bottom and put a slight bend into the quiver tip when all is tightened. Upstream bites are usually positive and unmistakable: the tip flicks straight and the line falls slack, necessitating a wide arc of rod when striking.

Laying On

Although the river deepens again in the next 100yd, it holds too few roach for any spot to be classed as roachy. There are none of the nice steady glides that roach prefer to live in. But the outside bank of the first bend we come to is a different proposition. I call it Lazy Man's Bend because I go there when I feel like a relaxed session and do not fancy working too hard for my fish. I can take it easy because the bend holds a better class of roach, and bigger roach do not usually come to the net one after another. The fish live there throughout the season except when flood water drives them across the river to shelter behind the bed of silt lying below the inside of the bend.

The current has scoured a 9ft deep run close in to the bank, and the best way to fish it is the much neglected laying on method using a 12 or 13ft rod with a peacock quill float set at a little over 10ft deep so that the hook length lies on the bottom. Enough shot is bunched about 3½ft above the hook to just cock the float. Then the bottom shot in the string, usually a No. 1 or BB, is slid down far enough for it to sit on the bottom. The float now lies at half cock, bites registering when it falls flat or glides along the surface before going under. The quality roach here respond well to light groundbaiting with mashed bread. Flake is the best hookbait.

The second bend of the 'S' is similar to the first in that it also contains roach, but since it curves in the opposite direction with the flow hitting the far bank and scouring out a deep channel, the roach are now at longer range on the other side of the river. Laying on is no longer practical because the current between rod tip and float would drag the bait out of position. In flood water, the hotspot is the slack behind the silt bed, just around the bend on our bank. Laying on there becomes viable in the right conditions.

Swimfeeder Legering

I leger the far bank swim using tactics similar to those of the first pool but with 4lb reel line and a small block end feeder instead of the lead when maggots are the bait. An open end feeder loaded with moistened white crumb is used when breadflake, crust or worms are on the hook. Adding a few free samples of hookbait to the crumb accustoms roach to accepting hook-sized pieces.

Most shop-bought feeders do not empty quickly enough because the holes are too small. A half-full feeder retrieved across the river scatters groundbait all over the place instead of where you want it in the swim, so if your feeder still holds bait after five minutes, its holes should be enlarged. Carefully positioned groundbait is one of the most important aspects of river fishing whatever the species.

Ringing the changes with bait presentation picks up bonus fish. You can try shortening the hook link to just a few inches when fishing a block end feeder, and using crust or punched bread on a size 14 hook. Both baits are buoyant enough to rise above the bottom and lie suspended above the feeder. The feeder holes are enlarged and the body is filled with a fifty-fifty mixture of semi-dry crumb and sausage rusk. Rusk is so buoyant that particles pop out of the feeder and float upward past the hookbait.

Bait Flavourings

Another dodge for those willing to experiment is to flavour groundbait and/or the hookbait with concentrated liquid flavouring available from suppliers of carp baits. Those I have used successfully include caramel, bun spice, nectar and butterscotch, though many others may be equally effective I suppose. Add the flavour to water – about 10ml to ½gall – then blend in the dry groundbait. Crust is treated by soaking a couple of cloths in flavoured water, wringing out the surplus, then sandwiching the crust between them. Finally, weigh down the package with a flat, heavy board and leave it overnight. Compressed, flavoured crust is a superb hookbait. I like to pull off suitable sized pieces, leaving a naturally jagged edge. The hook is inserted once through the middle.

Locating Hotspots

The long straight below the 'S' bend is classic roach water, the stream gliding smoothly over a level bottom nearly 6ft deep between rush-lined banks. The section offers perfect trotting, in my view the

(Opposite) It looks like an exceptional river roach, but in fact it is a roach/bream hybrid.

method that gives more enjoyment than any other whatever the species – though I would not mind betting it was originally devised by some imaginative angler who had roach in mind.

Outwardly, the whole straight looks like one roachy glide, and indeed it is. However, certain spots still produce better catches, one being a small depression in the river bed just a few inches deeper than its surroundings. Little features like this have to be pinpointed by trial and error with a plummet but are well worth the effort involved. Whilst plumbing this stretch I located a clean gravel area. I felt the plummet scrape over the hard bottom instead of mud – the feeling transmitted through the rod is quite distinct. Roach love gravel in a medium depth swim, so this patch is probably the best swim of the whole fishery.

Bulrushes may provide a clue to gravel's location because they usually grow on fairly firm bottoms, sometimes sandy shingle, sometimes alongside a gravel bank. These are the dark green, thin, round stem variety not to be confused with other rushes that grow profusely in mud and silt. Silkweed is another hotspot in-

Winter float fishing in a mill backwater.

A lone roach from a summer swim. It is unusual to take more than one or two fish in such conditions.

dicator. Who knows why roach like it? Perhaps they are partial to the weed itself, for at times they can be caught on strands of it; more likely the abundance of larvae and snails that silkweed contains holds the key. Whatever the case may be, a patch of silkweed in a steady flow usually has roach close to it.

As I have said, roach like low light. That is why the overhanging willows on the far bank conceal a good sized shoal. So do the submerged lily leaves waving in the current at the end of the straight. Cabbages they are called due to their resemblance to that vegetable. I think roach like them because of the security they offer, their shade, and the moderate current. Laying on with stronger line or allowing a free falling nip of flake to flutter down under a self-cocking float are two of the best ways I know to extract roach from cabbages. The fish are usually of a good stamp.

Trotting

The other hotspots we have covered on this straight stretch respond best to trotting with a 12–13ft match-type rod, 2lb line, 1.7lb hook length and hook size appropriate to the chosen bait – an 18 to start with for maggot and caster, a 16 or 14 for small pinches of flake.

On calm days or into an upstream breeze my preference is for a wire stemmed stick float. Provided it is well shotted down, a large one carrying four or five BBs can be used. A big float gives superior stability and tackle control as it rides down the

Travel light – this is all the tackle you need.

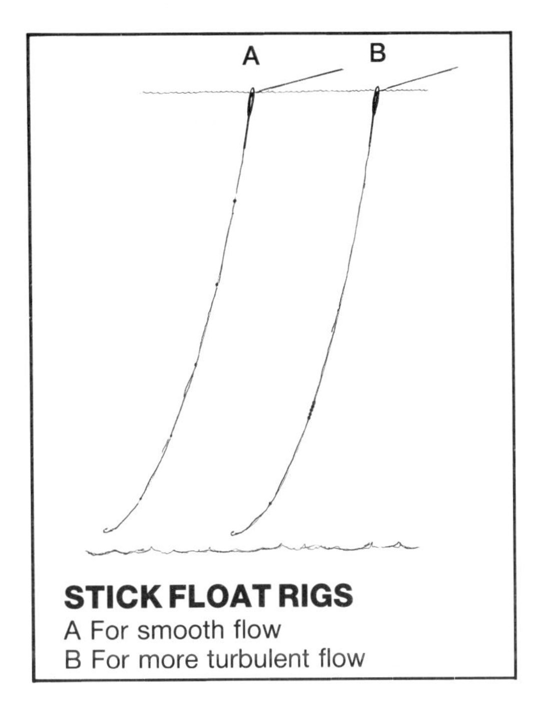

stream and is especially useful when you mend line. Stick floats are pushed along too quickly in a downstream wind and thus create unnatural bait presentation. A waggler fixed bottom end only is then a lot better. The stronger the wind, the longer the waggler should be so that line between float and rod tip is well submerged and unaffected by the wind.

Many anglers claim to trot effectively with a fixed spool reel. I can only admire their skill since I find them poor tools for the job. Excessive line twist, poor spillage from the spool and the necessity to trap the line with your forefinger before striking, then having to close the bale arm once the fish is hooked are all unacceptable to me. A closed face reel is better though the inadequate gearing gives poor line retrieve and handling when the rod is under load, such as when a big fish is hooked.

A free running centre-pin knocks both into a cocked hat when it comes to trotting, allowing perfect control over the float's progress by feathering the revolving drum with your finger or thumb to produce just the right amount of line tension. Admittedly they are not the easiest reels to cast with, though for trotting up to two rod lengths out casting is not required anyway. The tackle is simply swung out. Those who master the art of casting longer

(Opposite) A good bag in the ½–1½lb class.

distances will find the centre pin perfect for far bank trotting in medium sized rivers as well. Long casts are made by either pulling off successive loops of line from between the rod rings and then releasing them during the forward cast, or by setting the spool spinning with a flick of the rim and simultaneously swinging out the tackle so that line is pulled neatly through the rod rings. Spinning the reel too fast produces overruns; too slow a reel impedes the float which falls short of the mark.

Do not load a centre pin with too much line. Overlaid coils tend to dig into those beneath, giving poor line flow; 50yd is ample for any roach swim. Loading the line on backwards improves its flow because then it leaves the top of the reel instead of the bottom and thus passes straight into the butt ring. Friction is much less than when the reel is loaded the usual way around. Line billowing between reel and butt ring can be a problem in strong winds, but you can reduce it with an extra ring placed about 12in from the reel.

5 *Bream*

River bream are peculiar fish, the most difficult to understand of all river species, I think. Some days they come to net so easily that you get the impression a bright chimpanzee could catch them. Other times you try everything you know to tempt one fish from a shoal that is obviously feeding but steadfastly refuses to have anything to do with the hookbait. Yet other days produce a bite every throw: bold, unmissable bites which nonetheless are inexplicably missed one after another.

HABITAT AND BEHAVIOUR

Bream are generally associated with deep, slow stretches of river but they also do well in the upper reaches and smaller tributaries and are becoming increasingly widespread in faster currents such as those of southern chalk streams. Weirpools often contain a resident shoal or two, and at times they can be caught even in the white water. But it is the wide placid reaches of lowland river which contain the most worthwhile shoals, East Anglian streams notably providing some of the best bream fishing of all. The unhurried environment suits the bream's nature, which is just as placid as where it lives. Even on the hook they seem in no hurry to escape.

The species is criticised for its lack of fighting spirit; but of course they are not built for power and their weakness is amply compensated for by their bulk and numbers – you can soon fill a keepnet with bream. In any case, their faintheartedness applies only in sluggish water. Bream hooked from clear flowing upper reaches soon silence the critics, fighting with the tenacity of a tench or chub of the same size.

My first experience of hard-fighting bream came years ago during a chub session on an overgrown tiny river. I thought that chub would be lying in the fastish shallow gravel run under the trailing branches of a willow on the far bank. I legered a large wodge of flake there and watched the tip for bites. After a while the tip walloped round and I struck into a heavy 'chub' which forced me to yield line as it bolted powerfully downstream. Right up to the net I still thought it was a chub, and could hardly believe it when a singularly handsome bream surfaced before me, the first of a bag of equally immaculate fish from that apparently unlikely bream swim.

That's another thing about bream from upper rivers and similar purer environments. Not only do they scrap, but they are better looking, cleaner-handling fish with broad shoulders and lacking the thick slime typical of slow water bream. I presume that the slime affords some protection in the more polluted, parasite-infested reaches of middle and lower rivers.

Bream are a true shoal fish. There may be three or three hundred together. If one feeds, they all feed; if one moves, they all move. They are also perfect pike fodder. I have read that their flat 'tea tray' shape has evolved so that bream can more easily weave their way through submerged rush beds where they find sanctuary from their

Groundbait is essential for success with bream.

tormentors. I think that is nonsense – in all my days of fishing I have yet to see or hear about bream found amongst rushes, except on isolated occasions when they were spawning. In fact, their flat shape evolved to allow them to pack more tightly together when danger threatens. Those deep flanks are adapted to give a large area of mirror camouflage, for beneath the water bream reflect perfectly the surroundings they happen to be in, as do other shiny, scaled species. The bream's only defences are camouflage and numbers. A pike feeds by stalking a shoal, selecting and lunging at a chosen individual fish. I can well imagine it being disoriented when confronted by a milling group of mirrored tea trays.

My experiences with fast-water bream were exceptions to the rule. Nine times out of ten you are more likely to locate them in the deeper, slower sections, in holes, pools, slacks and eddies, in quiet water out of the main flow with a mud or clay bottom. This highlights another peculiarity of the species: they are the only fish mentioned in the book that seem to prefer a soft bottom to one of clean gravel.

Location

Locating fish is not so much a question of finding a likely stretch as pinpointing the whereabouts of the shoal in that particular area. In summer the problem may be resolved easily because it is common to see a whole shoal basking just beneath the surface, the occasional dorsal fin waggling in the air and the odd vortex as a bream swirls. It is an impressive sight particularly when the shoal numbers several hundred fish.

On those days bream dangle before you like the proverbial carrot before a donkey, for although I have taken a few basking fish from still waters I have never been in the least successful on rivers. The shoals may feed on the river bed directly underneath their basking area, but more often they move a short way up or down stream before getting their heads down. The best strategy is to prebait a swim adjacent to the shoal – not so close as to disturb them – then settle down to fish when the sun loses its heat and sends the bream deeper. If they

(Opposite) A typical shoal bream in the 5lb class.

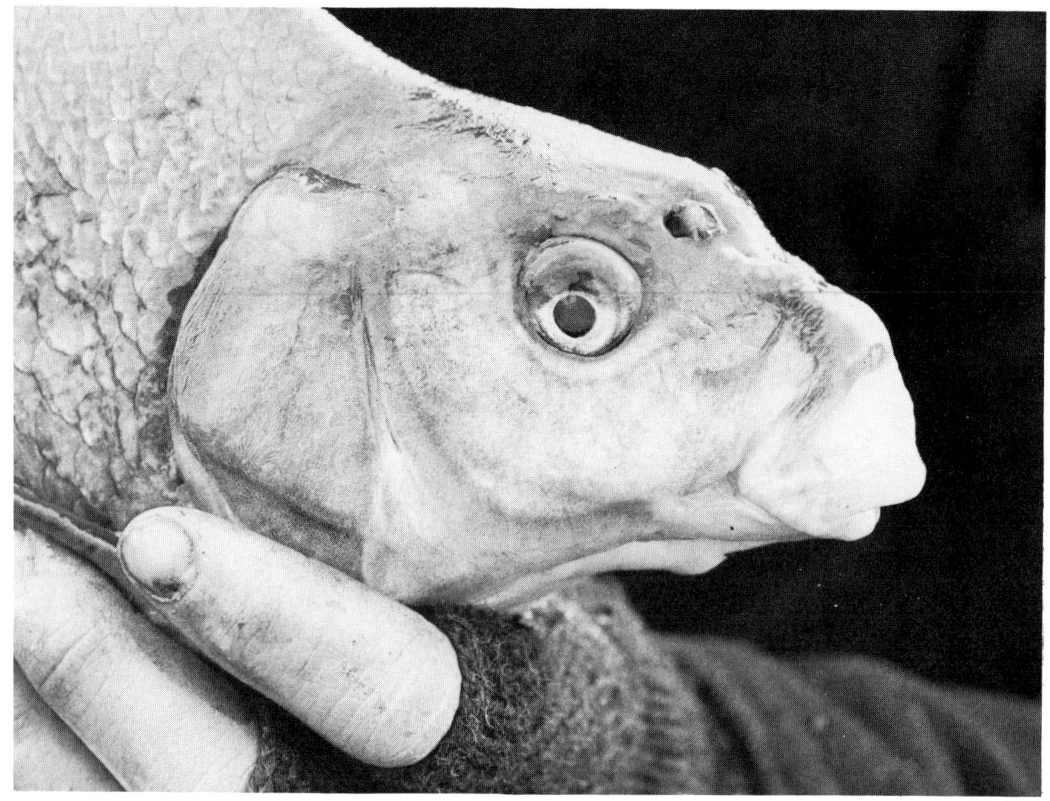

Telescopic jaws grub food from the river bed.

feed at all there is every chance that they will home in on your baited patch.

Rolling bream reveal another clue about where to fish. Dawn and dusk are the most reliable times to watch bream roll, although in muggy weather they may continue throughout the day. A good chop on the water does not appear to encourage river bream as it does in still water; in fact you are more likely to see river bream when not a ripple disturbs the surface.

It is important to know that bream roll in two different ways depending upon what they are doing. When feeding, they lollop over and make a considerable boil as they do so. Usually you can spot their broad flanks, and sometimes the tail clears the surface then smacks the water as the fish flops over. When you see bream rolling like that you're in business.

The second type of rolling is very different, easily distinguished and marks the fish as travellers on the move to another feeding or resting area. They slice through the water, head, shoulders, dorsal fin and upper lobe of the tail cutting through the surface, usually so quietly that you miss the shoal unless you happen to be looking in the right place. I have known the odd fish accept a slow falling bait offered in front of a moving shoal, but you are better off following at a safe distance to try to find out where they are going. Following the shoal's movement is easy enough when they come to the surface regularly. They all head in the same direction. Mind you, where they cease coming up is not necessarily where they have chosen to feed or rest. Sometimes bream keep moving so deep that you cannot spot them.

In autumn dace shoals move into deeper swims, where they can be caught on trotted baits.

Barbel are probably the most prized of coarse fish. Extremely shy and hard-fighting, they haunt dense weed beds and gravel runs in clear, fast flowing rivers.

Roach and bream sometimes cross-breed. The result is a powerful, heavy, 'roachy'-looking fish that is often difficult to identify from the pure-bred species.

Middle and lower rivers, slow moving and muddy, are the natural haunt of bream. They are poor fighters, but make spectacular match weights.

Roach fishing in late autumn is a high spot in the river fisherman's calendar.

The record 10lb 2oz Suffolk Stour zander, caught on deadbait by Doug Wood.

Since disease hit British waters, nets of specimen perch have been a rarity. Now they are on the way back, much to the river fisherman's delight.

River pike are smaller than those from stillwater, but much faster, more powerful fighters. Live and deadbait tactics score in winter, especially when the fish shoal in preparation for spawning.

Two friends of mine once devised an effective method of locating a particularly elusive shoal in a featureless stretch of river. They 'leapfrogged' along the bank using swingtip leger tackle, but without hook and bait. An odd way to catch bream, you'd think but the plan worked well. The idea was to alternate their way through the swims by casting across the river, pausing and retrieving until either the swim had been thoroughly searched without result or produced line bites, which indicated they had found the bream. With the spot marked, they went back for the rest of their tackle. Their good thinking was usually rewarded with a nice bag of fish.

Bubblers

Bubbles and areas of coloured water are sure signs of feeding. Anglers love to argue about how and why all kinds of fish make bubbles. I have even heard the opinion that the bubbles break forth from the fish's vent! But of course bubbles are caused when a feeding fish sucks up gases trapped in the bottom along with muck and food.

Depth and flow are important features of a bream swim. Get to know your local hotspots.

The gases are expelled through the back of the gill rakers and rise to the surface as bubbles. The size of the bubbles is controlled by the structure of the gill rakers; the more numerous the rakers, the smaller the bubbles. Tench have many rakers and thus produce a mass of tiny bubbles when gases are sieved through their gills. I have never examined a bream's rakers but as their bubbles are pea-sized I suppose they have relatively few. You may see half a dozen bubbles or a great patch depending upon how vigorously the fish roots through the bottom and upon how much gas is trapped there.

In clearer summer conditions the bottom-rummaging of bream so discolours the area that it can be seen clearly, and this is obviously the place to fish. Remember to allow for the rate of flow before putting in your bait though. The discoloured water is always downstream of the exact feeding zone. Where you find bream one day is not necessarily where they will be the next. They are habitual nomads and their wandering appears more frequent in summer than in winter. Cold water prompts them to take up residence in a comfortable, usually deep spot in which they remain unless floods or very mild weather spur them to move. Summer fish are like sheep: they graze an area for a while, perhaps a day, perhaps even a fortnight or more, before they eat themselves out of house and home and thus find it necessary to travel on. A regularly baited swim will hold the shoal for much longer, even indefinitely. The key word is regularly – miss a few days and you may return to a vacant swim.

Line bites are common wherever a shoal is moving about in a swim. They are most often encountered on leger rigs and are due to the bream bushing or swimming into the line, causing false reactions on float or indicator. Once you have found the shoal, *when* to fish for the bream is governed by the weather and light conditions, as it is with most river species. Like roach, bream feed best in low light. Much of the best river fishing is confined to early and late in the day, and throughout daylight should skies be overcast. Warm summer nights may produce the best sport of all on some rivers but not on others. As I say, bream are difficult to understand.

Winter breaming is best restricted to the mild spells or when rain injects extra colour into the river. A mild period coinciding with a flush of coloured water – com-

A pale fish from heavily clouded water.

(Opposite) Big bream are a matchman's dream.

ABU

Maggots and casters are good all-round baits for feeder work.

mon enough in most winters – is an opportunity not to be missed by any keen bream angler. Whether bream feed after dark in winter is something I have never discovered, though I have no doubt that the nocturnal bream enthusiast would do well to try.

Baits

Match and some specialist anglers excepted, I cannot help noticing that most fishermen are decidedly sloppy about the quality of bait they are willing to use. Good bait is vital for any species, and none more so than for bream. However, provided the quality is there bream will take a whole variety of baits, my favourites being a cocktail of red worms and maggots, or maggots and flake. They are closely followed in preference by red worms alone, maggots, casters, flake, crust and punched bread. It is curious that a cocktail bait frequently works when either bait alone, or any other, is rejected. Brandlings, those small red worms with yellowish rings and a pungent odour, are often recommended but are a poor substitute for proper red worms. Brandlings are found in the bottom layers of old pig manure or compost heaps. Reds are more selective: heaps of well rotted horse manure are the best places to dig them. Marsh worms are even better than reds, about twice the size, lively, similar colour, but difficult to find in numbers. You may discover a few by turning over old riverside logs or by digging in marshy areas of bankside vegetation where that is allowed.

Bream suck in and blow out a bait sever-

Quiver tip and target board.

Bream are delicate, and they don't fight hard. But as compensation, you can take massive hauls.

al times before swallowing or rejecting it. The poorer the bait, the higher the chances of eventual rejection. Red worms remain fairly lively if stored in some of the manure from which you dug them. Maggots straight from the shop definitely need to be cleaned. Drop them into a riddle containing bran or bread crumbs moistened with a little milk, and let the maggots work their way through the meshes to fall into a container beneath. Repeat the process two or three times for best results.

Specials are the best maggots to use. Bream find plump, soft gozzers irresistible. You are unlikely to be able to buy them because they are hard to breed in commercial numbers. Breed your own instead: gozzers are just the larvae of bluebottles fed on pigeon meat. If you cannot get pigeon, a pig's heart from the butcher will do. Good specials can be bred from chicken.

All you need is a large tin with a few big holes punched in the lid. Place the pigeon inside – preferably it should be 'high' already – and leave the tin in a shady spot for a day until the meat is fly-blown. You will see clusters of creamy coloured eggs on the meat. Remove the pigeon and wrap it in plenty of newspaper. After three or four days the maggots should be about half grown. Add more meat if necessary, then leave for a further four or five days. Riddle the maggots as described above.

Flavoured maggots work well for bream, and although I have yet to try it I see no reason why the flavour could not be imparted by adding it to the meat upon which the maggots are bred. Carp-type special pastes are nowhere near as effective for bream as they are for other species. I once caught a number of bream on shrimp concentrate based paste from a swim prebaited for tench. However, I would probably have caught them on more conventional baits as well.

Groundbaiting

Thoughtful groundbaiting is every bit as important as good quality hookbait. The well-worn advice about lots of feed for bream holds true only on big, heavily populated rivers. I would advise considerably more caution about baiting on small and medium rivers where quality, smell and method of feeding are vastly more important than how many bucketfuls are tipped in.

An excellent groundbait for attracting and holding bream consists of 60 per cent white bread crumb, 20 per cent layer's mash and 20 per cent of a smelly concoction of fish blood and bone meal (the latter two ingredients are available from animal food merchants). Add the dry mix to water (flavoured to match the hookbait if necessary) to obtain a firm mixture that breaks up on the bottom, not as it hits the surface or even at half depth. If the ball breaks up too soon, two things happen: much of the food drifts downstream in the current, perhaps taking the bream with it, and it encourages bream to feed off the bottom as they rise to intercept the falling particles. They can be caught on slowly falling or trotted baits, but bream are much easier to hook when they feed hard on the bottom. That is where you must concentrate the groundbait for best results.

The holding quality of the mix is enhanced by the addition of feed maggots, casters, chopped worms, nips of flake or other samples of hookbait. Squats are the best shoal holders I know – use as many as can be crammed into the mix without ruining its binding properties. Pinkies or ordinary maggots are considerably inferior because the groundbait will not bind properly, and anyway the maggots tend to creep out of sight in the river bed debris. When only pinkies and others are available, I scald them in boiling water. Put

Note the length of the hook tail – the bait is more than 3ft from the feeder.

them in a fine meshed sieve and pour the water over them whereupon the maggots stretch to nearly twice normal length, turn pale and no longer creep around.

Good sport is better assured on any river by prebaiting a swim for a few days before-hand. Big shoals in big rivers need a correspondingly enthusiastic prebaiting campaign, topped up during the fishing session in accordance with how the shoal feeds. When the bream feed heavily, add groundbait frequently and liberally. If sport is slow, further heavy groundbait is unlikely to improve matters.

The bream of medium and small rivers respond better to a reasonable dose, say five or six balls when you start fishing, followed by careful topping up with small balls or by loose feeding with maggots, etc. The latter method encourages midwater feeding, unfortunately. If I know there are bream already feeding in a small river swim, I refrain from groundbaiting at all until the action slows down. Even then I bait sparingly and carefully, for I have seen many a shoal so alarmed by heavy bombardment that they leave the swim.

TACTICS AND TECHNIQUES

The mood of the bream and the type of river and swim dictate which method to use. Big rivers call for swimfeeder tactics which help to top up the groundbait and keep it all in the right spot. Swimfeeding can work on smaller rivers as well, but I confine them to deeper swims and coloured water. I have seen fish spooked by feeders splashing into clear water. Mostly I prefer to do without, preferring a simple paternoster leger rig with a long hooktail. A leger rod for feeder fishing needs backbone to handle the weight: try a medium action 10 –12 footer of 1lb test curve and matched to 4lb main line plus a lighter hook link. For straight legering a lighter rod of the same easy action is more suitable, with a 2½–3lb reel line and light link. Either rod may be fitted with a threaded tip ring accepting a screw-in swing, spring or quiver tip. In my view a ready spliced quiver beats all.

A very long hook link is of importance when you are legering for bream. Long tails allow a more natural bait presentation and that helps to reduce the suspicious suck–blow routine. Hook points should always be honed needle-sharp and protrude from the bait so that there is every chance of the point taking hold as the bait is blown out. When that happens bream wallop the rod tip round like chub.

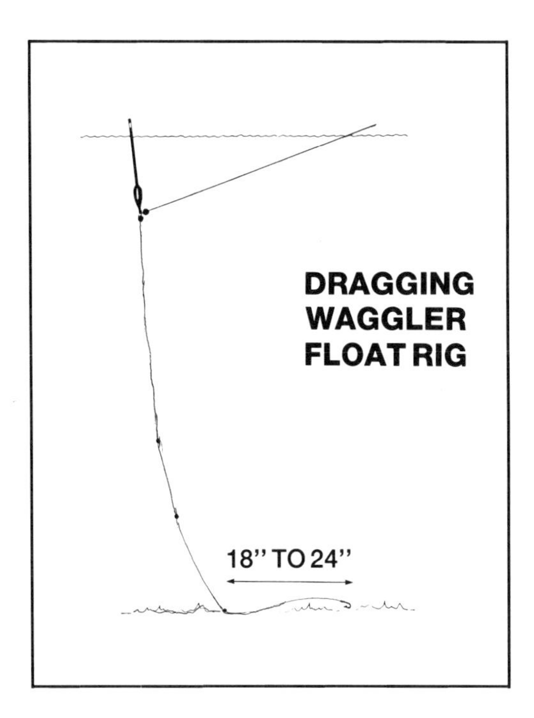

The prick of the hook makes it bolt. On the other hand, bites can be so incredibly small that great concentration is required to see any indication at all.

I recall occasions when barely ¼in movements of the quiver tip have resulted in good catches, the bream usually hooked well inside the mouth. Bream often give small bites even though they are feeding confidently. Sometimes, especially when you are loose feeding, the bait is intercepted as it sinks. A bite is easily missed if you are not watching for it, so after casting, stop the line flowing from the reel immediately the leger hits the water; now the rig sinks on a tight line to the rod tip, and when the leger hits bottom the pressure on the line is reduced and it falls slack. You soon get used to the time it takes for this to happen. A bite is recognised by the line staying tight to the rod instead of falling slack at the expected time.

When flow is not too strong and distances are small, it is effective to lay on with a 12 or 13ft match rod and float tackle, presenting the stationary bait which bream tend to prefer. At the same time, bites are positive and detected early. It is also aesthetically a nicer method for those who like to watch a float.

Feeding bream tilt their heads downwards to take a bait. Amid much tail waving, they are likely to foul a line lying straight up and down between float and river bed and thus produce false indications. With a number of bream feeding in the area there is no obvious remedy except legering, but you can reduce the problem by allowing a long length of line to lie along the bottom between hook and shot, an arrangement that in any case produces more confident bites because the bream feels less resistance.

Special Techniques

When you get lovely sailaway bites yet miss every strike, it sometimes pays to increase the tackle's resistance. To understand why this happens, consider how a bream feeds. Its lips can be extended like a telescope, a facility it uses to suck in baits from an inch or more distant. Sometimes, for reasons that only a bream can answer, the bait is merely sucked to the extreme outer edges of the lips and held there. Perhaps the bream is suspicious; perhaps the bait is poor. Whatever the cause, the strike misses for the simple reason that hook and bait were not in the mouth at all.

I believe that Cheshire bream angler Graham Marsden first suggested that increasing the resistance may provide a solution. The theory is that upon taking up a little free line the bream then feels the bait about to be pulled from its mouth by the resistance. It feels obliged to take a better grip, which it does by sucking the bait further into its mouth.

In practice the method does work, but not always. Instead of taking a tighter grip, the bream may decide to spit out the bait. But the trick pays off often enough to be worth a try when you keep missing

Handle with care – bream are easily damaged.

bites. Increase the resistance by adding more shot when laying on, and by allowing the line to tighten and the tip to bend into the bite when legering.

Generally speaking, the only movement I like in a bottom fished bait is when I tweak it along a few inches. This often prompts the bream to bite. Other than that I think a static bait is better. There are sometimes exceptions, often coinciding with an extra push of water along the river, when a trotted bait is more effective. However, the bait should be fished to travel through the swim at less than the current's rate. It is best running at little more than a crawl, this is achieved by setting the float overdepth so that about 24in of hooktail drags along the bottom behind the float. Swim depth must be plumbed accurately and the bottom shot set just to drag the river bed. A waggler float with buoyant antenna of peacock quill or sarkandas reed, fixed bottom end only, is best. The dragging shot repeatedly catches on the river bed and is pulled into the debris, so the float is slightly undershotted to provide an extra bit of buoyancy to counteract the problem by lifting the shot free.

As the float drifts downstream it slowly dips as the drag shot catches, pops up again and continues down. Bites are easily distinguished from this natural dragging action. The float either lifts or slides under and away positively. Larger floats carrying more shot can be used when the water is choppy, but in really rough conditions the method is ruled out. On the right day, though, drag-trotting can be deadly. Because depth setting is crucial to success, it is a sound policy to measure the position of the float by aligning it with the rod rings. Should you break off, the float can be reset exactly right.

Handling the Catch

Treat your bream with care. They are extremely fragile fish, prone to disease and fungus when their protective layer of slime is displaced. I sometimes despair on seeing a packed keepnet hauled ashore, the bream red and sore from continually rubbing themselves against the meshes. Those at the bottom are badly crushed and unlikely to survive. It is a fact of fishing that many anglers like to admire the whole catch at the end of the session, but do spare a thought for bream and consider slipping them back one by one as you catch them. If you must keep them, use several large keepnets instead of one.

6 *Dace*

If dace weighed 3–4lb, I have little doubt that they would be at the top of many a river angler's list of favourite species. But of course they do not grow so big: a half pounder is a good one, yet still a relatively little fish. Thus dace tend to take a back seat compared to larger-growing river fish except to some discerning anglers who have discovered that what dace lack in weight is certainly compensated for in spirit. Size for size they fight as hard as any chub.

HABITAT AND BEHAVIOUR

Dace fans also appreciate that where they are found, shoals are quite big. Almost to the extent of chub they are prepared to continue feeding merrily when river conditions have ruled out sport with the more temperature conscious species. Offhand I cannot think of a river anywhere in Britain where dace do not occur, though in the middle and lower reaches of slow flowing streams the shoals tend to be rather isolated and take some finding. On the whole, dace prefer shallow, cleaner, swift-flowing sections.

As rivers are subjected to more and more abstraction, so flow rates fall, resulting in a deterioration in the quality of dace fishing compared to that of several decades ago. Nowadays the upper reaches of rivers, sidestreams and small tributaries are far better places to look for quality shoals.

Above the main areas of pollution, the river is characterised by a livelier and more consistent flow. It runs clearer and cleaner over greener and more luxuriant weedbeds, and there are plenty of glides, gravelly shallows, small pools and tree-lined runs – the perfect habitat for dace.

Specimen Dace

You may think it strange that while I deliberately refrain from writing about ways to catch larger than average specimens of other species, I feel compelled to emphasise the capture of bigger than normal dace. I make their small size my excuse. Whatever the reason, those intimate headwaters and sidestreams are the best spots to seek out the better shoals which may well have dace averaging 8 –10oz or more depending on the river's quality.

Dace over a pound, once an attainable target on many rivers, are becoming almost as scarce as mermaids. The current record fish weighed 1lb 4oz 4dr and was caught from the Little Ouse near Thetford in 1960. Larger fish than that have been recorded, including the one-time record held by R.W. Humphries at 1lb 8oz 5dr, hooked from a tributary of the Hampshire Avon in 1932. (The fish was removed from the record list in 1969 due to insufficient proof of its capture.) The Bedford Ivel once produced huge dace such as L. Cookson's specimen of 1lb 8oz, and the Eden in Carlisle produced a 1lb 6oz fish.

Being realistic I have to conclude that it seems unlikely the record will ever be broken, yet there are still a few rivers capable of springing a surprise and certainly able to produce dace of over a pound. Even the Little Ouse could do the trick. Other rivers include the Norfolk streams

Creep along the banks and stay low to avoid spooking the shoal.

Thet, Wensum, Tud and Tas, the Berkshire Kennet, the Herefordshire Wye, some of the Hampshire chalk streams and my home river the Suffolk Stour, at one time a Mecca for outsize dace and still holding a few big fish in some stretches.

Most specimen dace I have heard about were caught by accident, usually by an angler fishing for roach or chub in slower deeper runs than those generally preferred by ordinary dace. The biggest specimens tend to isolate themselves from smaller shoal fish, and the spots to look for them are deeper glides, pools and slacks, preferably overhung with branches or vegetation. Perhaps they think they are chub!

Little chub are often mistaken for large dace, I recall a classic example when Pete, a fishing friend, legered for chub after dark one very cold winter's night. Baiting with a chub-sized lump of cheesepaste he had one belter of a bite. His strike met only token resistance from an apparently very small chub, which was unceremoniously wound in splashing back across the surface, lifted from the water, unhooked and was about to be thrown back into the pitch dark river when Pete noticed a decidedly un-chublike feel about it. Torchlight revealed a dace nudging the one pound mark.

Even in daylight there is confusion between small chub and big dace, for there is so close a similarity that at first glance many anglers are fooled into thinking they have caught a specimen dace. A second look will show clearly that they have clear identification points. The anal and dorsal fins of the dace are distinctly concave, while the chub's are convex. The dace's ventral and anal fins are pale coral pink instead of orange/red like the chub's. The dace's tail is a translucent pale green; the chub's is dark grey, sometimes nearly black. In any case, the slim delicate shape, narrow head, large eye and small mouth of the dace characterises the species quite well enough if you compare it to the thick-bodied chub with its broad head, thick lips and large mouth.

TACTICS AND TECHNIQUES

Summer dace fishing on small rivers can be frustrating but enormous fun. Most minor streams are little fished, and consequently untrodden and heavily overgrown so that an angler is likely to find himself crawling around among nettles and bracken as he attempts to sneak up on a shoal. Dace are extremely difficult to approach without

Small looking fish, but these dace are close to specimen weight.

triggering the alarm and scattering the shoal. With utmost caution it is possible to inch your way into place well upstream and, by sending a few maggots or casters downstream, to get the shoal darting about in the current to intercept them.

Once they are seen to be feeding confidently, a trotted bait on 1½lb line beneath a tiny float will tempt one fish, rarely two, but hardly ever three before the shoal becomes visibly agitated and finally departs the swim amid frantic bow waves. Summer dace are great opportunist feeders that readily intercept all sorts of insects, grubs, caterpillars and berries (especially elderberries) as they are carried down in the flow. Sometimes these natural baits outfish more normal offerings like maggots or casters, and they work particularly well if the fish are a bit choosy. There is great satisfaction in leaving the maggots at home and relying on what baits can be rummaged from the bankside.

Summer dace fishing is very much the same as chubbing in that the fisherman will do better to keep mobile, travelling light and taking a dace or two from each swim as it is located. Generally, dace of a size shoal together so that in one swim

Dace are far more streamlined than roach.

Hunting summer dace. Stay mobile, and travel light.

there will be nothing above a few ounces, yet the next may often hold much larger fish. If the water is clear enough, you can bypass the babies and concentrate on the specimens.

By donning waders and getting into the water you can avoid upsetting the dace too much. Because you are under the skyline and below the angle of the fish's vision, you will not be seen so easily if you keep your head down, wade quietly and approach from downstream – that is, from behind the fish which lie with their heads to the current.

Flyfishing

Flyfishing is for me the most enjoyable way to fish, and one of the most effective as well. Dace rise freely to artificials and provided care is taken the shoal may not prove so timid as usual. Sometimes several fish can be hooked from the same spot.

You *could* catch dace on an AFTM 10 reservoir fly rod, but such over gunning will dampen the dace's fighting spirit and spoil the fun. A nice flexible rod 7–8ft long and balanced to a 3 or 4 weight line is far more appropriate. Match the rod to a double taper floating line which allows accurate short range casting and featherlight delivery of the fly on to the surface. A splashy cast on heavy tackle is almost guaranteed to clear the swim before you can hook a single fish.

I like to use as long a leader as I can safely cast, though branches in the casting area and other obstructions are the limiting factor on small streams. Wind also limits the safe leader length, but I still

Dace feed where the current runs under the fallen tree.

recommend at least 8–9ft whenever possible. A long leader reduces the chances of an inaccurate cast dropping the flyline instead of the leader on top of the dace. That also is sure to spook the shoals. I find it convenient to buy ready-made tapered leaders, but it is easy enough to make your own by knotting together lines of reducing diameter to produce the right taper. I prefer a point breaking strain of about 3lb.

Which Fly?

Dace take wet flies and artificial nymphs fished below the surface, but I would rather catch them on dry flies. Perhaps it is the enjoyment of making a perfectly judged cast and watching the floating fly drift downstream towards me, then seeing it disappear in the splashy ring of a dace's rise. The fly's pattern does not matter very much provided it alights, floats and travels downstream naturally. Presentation is far more important than exact pattern. Most dace are taken on small flies tied on hooks size 16 –12, though there are times when bigger flies also work well. Observe the sizes of any naturals that are hatching or are being blown into the water, then match your fly size to them.

Although, as I say, fly pattern is not critical, dace do often show some preference for something black. If I had to choose one fly and size it would be 16 black gnat. Besides black, small brown flies like Coachman, Alder and Coch-y-Bondhu will catch plenty of dace.

Treat the leader with floatant to within a few inches of the point, and the fly as well. Approach the shoal, keeping yourself low, wading without disturbing the water – and taking care to avoid disappearing with a shriek into any unsuspected deep hole.

Cast upstream and diagonally across to the shoal and, as the fly rides down with the flow towards you, recover loose line but be careful not to affect the fly's natural progress. Dace usually rise to a surface fly with a resounding splash likely to startle the angler just enough to make him miss the bite. Delayed strikes nearly always miss this quick-biting species, but after a few swims and a few takes your reflexes sharpen and you will start to hook fish. However, you never will hit them all: dace

(Opposite) Above average Stour dace hooked on trotted maggot.

Winter dace swim.

fly fishermen are philosophical about missed fish – it is all part of the game.

With very accurate casts, and providing you can see the fish, it is possible to offer the fly to the dace nearest you. The hooked fish is drawn directly away from the shoal and with luck will not scare the rest. Casting first to the head of the shoal means playing the dace past the others, with obvious results. For similar reasons try not to let the dace splash as it fights. Keep the rod tip low, which pulls the fish down rather than up to the surface. However, dace are splashy little fellows and sometimes in shallow water can foil any attempt to make them behave themselves and come quietly.

Of course you do not have to use fly rods to fly fish for dace. Use a match rod and float to present a natural fly or any other type of insect. I well recall that one of my favourite pastimes as a lad was to stand on the bridge near Brundon Mill on the Stour trotting down big, speckled grey flies which I had caught as they sunned themselves on a wooden gate. Extracting them one at a time from the matchbox I kept them in was quite an art, and having one escape my fingers and buzz free was a disaster. They certainly took some catching. My chums and I soon discovered, cruelly I admit, that if we pulled off one wing, escapees just buzzed around in circles and we could grab them again. Fishing then was extremely basic, but would still work just as well today. No shot on the line, just a small float lying flat on the surface, fixed about 3ft from the fly on the hook. We let the tackle drift downstream to the waiting dace, who always obliged.

Winter Fishing

Flyfishing will take dace in the depths of winter too, but I neglect the method then for no other reason than that I would not enjoy it as much as I do in summer. Cold days are better spent trotting, a technique which is effective in both smaller streams and the wider stretches lower downriver. The extra colour and depth of the river in winter means that probably you cannot spot the shoals. One way to locate them is to feed a generous helping of floating casters downstream, whereupon anything like reasonable weather conditions should have the dace rising to the surface. If no fish appear, then the day is too cold and they are lying near the bottom of deeper, slower runs. A good rule of thumb for winter dace is to go for the shallows in milder weather, and fish the deep swims when it is really cold.

Trotting picks up large bags of dace on the right day, using similar tactics and baits to those of summer. Stronger currents demand suitably stepped up floats and more weight to provide the necessary control. Most swims can be loose-fed with free samples. Feed little and often – it is important to get the feeding rate just right.

Easily confused apart from weight – chub above, dace below.

Delicate features belie the dace's voracious lifestyle.

Overfeed and the hookbait is ignored; underfeed and you risk losing the shoal. A general rule is to feed liberally with maggots or casters until the dace are confidently accepting them, then reduce the rate to a dozen or more every trot down. If bites trail off and the fish have not been spooked, there is a good chance that too much feed is going into the river, so reduce it accordingly.

Coloured water and the additional flow of winter means that dace are not nearly as easily alarmed as they are in summer. They also seem little affected by water temperature and light intensity, often coming to net one after another on bright, cold days that invariably put off other river species. Strangely enough, dace usually stop feeding during the last hour of daylight, just about the time when roach start to come on. Which is very convenient for us.

(Opposite) Light trotting rod and closed face reel cope with general dace fishing.

7 Pike

My first pike rod was a makeshift contraption to say the least. I whipped the eye of a big safety pin to a 2in piece of dowel which I stuck into the ferrule of the second section of my prized general-purpose cane rod. My fishing mate went one better: he was lucky enough to own a proper pike rod. Well sort of, for it was labelled 'General Purpose Pike and Pier Rod' and had an action not unlike a garden hoe.

Gone are the days of poker-stiff rods and equally crude techniques. Now a huge army of pike fishermen specialise in the one species and, with this increase in the pike's status, have made many advances in tackle and techniques. More important, conservation and safe handling are key issues. Throughout the same period, the swing has been towards stillwaters – gravel pits especially – and one result is that a good deal of the sport available in our rivers remains largely unexploited.

In general it is true that stillwaters produce the biggest pike, not to mention the occasional huge river fish. A double figure specimen from any river is a fish to be pleased with. A twenty pounder is a great achievement – one that still evades me! Although they average a smaller size, river pike offer their own brand of appeal. They are leaner, fitter and they fight like demons winter and summer. Their stillwater counterparts do not fight anywhere near so hard in the colder months.

HABITAT AND BEHAVIOUR

River pike are easy to find because they live in swims that are predictable and fairly easy to recognise. Bends, slow wide stretches, slacks, holes, marginal rush beds and areas in and around weedbeds are generally worth exploring. Like chub, pike enjoy holing up in undercuts and beneath overhangs; unlike chub they prefer quiet water. Large slacks and slow eddies on the side of weirpools are very reliable.

Spots where tributaries or sidestreams enter the main river may hold pike in the last two months of the season when fish shoal up prior to spawning. They often move right up the feeder streams, though slack water each side of the entrance is more likely to be your best bet. You can also locate pike by talking to match fishermen who frequently are pestered by pike invading their swims to attack small fish.

The colouration and patterns on small and large pike shows that their camouflage changes as they grow. Small jacks have regular, stripy figurations on the flanks which provide superb camouflage among weeds and rush-lined swims. Bigger, older pike have mottled, blotchy flanks instead of stripes, which suggests they are camouflaged to hunt in open water dappled by light reflected from the water surface.

(Opposite) A good average river pike just shy of double figures.

Close range tactics – pike lie within a yard of the near bank.

Being sensible about it then, we anglers ought to concentrate on open water for river pike. Experience tells me there is some truth in this idea, but I have hooked enough big river fish from weed and rush swims to be a little wary of the theory. River pike are by no means always found in slacks and slow areas, for when feeding they obviously must hunt where the food fish live – sometimes in surprisingly fast water. I recall trotting baits down the white water of foaming weirpools with gates wide open, taking pike one after another.

I learned long ago that the sudden opening of floodgates can turn a dour day into one where pike are spurred into short but hectic feeding spells when it seems that every fish living immediately downstream of the gates is driven into a frenzy. I do not know why a sudden heavy push of water triggers the pikes' reaction. Perhaps they capitalise on the sudden activity of bait fish stirred up by the extra current.

Tackle

Unlike a stillwater pike fisherman, the river enthusiast does not need a combination of rods of different actions. A 10 –11ft rod f slow action and 2¼lb test curve is adequate for virtually every swim and any method. An exception is for fishing the far bank of a fast-moving river. Here a stiffer, longer rod is more suitable because it holds line high off the water and prevents the powerful midstream current from dragging tackle out of position.

Pike are not line shy so it pays to err on the safe side by loading the reel with

10 –12lb monofilament. Sylcast is popular because it is one of the toughest lines and well able to withstand the pressures of hard piking. Treble hooks in the range 10 –6 handle all my pike fishing. Partridge extra-strong outbends and the extra-strong Drennan patterns are among the best available. On barbed patterns, nip out two barbs of each treble, leaving the third for holding the bait. I believe I have never lost a pike through fishing barbless hooks; even if I had, the ease of unhooking and the satisfaction of knowing that a pike's jaws are not damaged would be well worth the occasional lost fish.

Ready-made traces complete with trebles can be bought but I never feel confident in them. I make my own instead, which is not only cheaper but far more

Traces stored neatly on a foam drum.

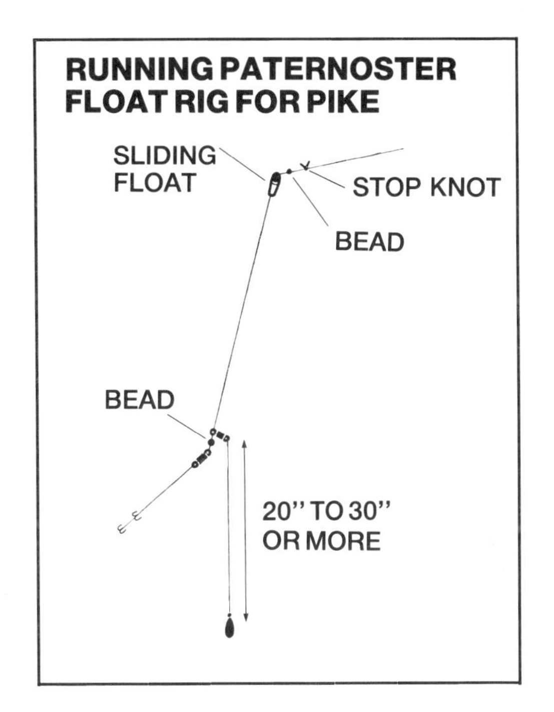

reliable. Marlin Steel is one of the best cable stainless wires on the market, and is less prone to kinking. It also twists up well for making traces. Kinks seriously weaken the trace and must be watched for, otherwise a big pike will discover the problem for you.

A few floats complete the basic equipment. Mine are sliders with either a swivel at the bottom or a hole through the centre. A slider can be locked into place on the line with stop knots or shot when a fixed float is required. Polystyrene balls (Polyballs) of 1in and 1½in diameters make economical and efficient pike floats and can be bought ready-bored and painted or plain for the do-it-yourself enthusiast.

Other bits and pieces include Berkeley or Drennan swivels, leads weighing up to 1½oz (1oz is the most useful), beads with small holes, and a good hook sharpening stone. The angler who fails to sharpen his hook points cannot complain when they fail to sink into the pike's hard, bony jaws.

Gaff and pike gags are definitely *not* needed. Neither has any place in the modern pike scene and should join the ranks of redundant hoe handle rods. A large landing net with small knitted meshes does minimal damage when you hoist fish on to the bank. Unhooking requires nothing more than a glove and large pair of forceps.

Livebaits are an emotive issue these days. It is the individual's decision to use them or not except in the few areas where livebaiting is banned already. Livebaits catch more pike than deads, and I use them when I must. I admit increasing pangs of guilt, now strong enough for me to seriously consider imposing my own personal ban. Deadbaits catch plenty of pike as well, with sprats a consistent catcher along with herrings, mackerel, smelt, sardines and freshwater species. Unusual sea fish are worth a try if you can get them and could well be effective when a stretch of water has been flogged with ordinary baits. Small whiting, whiting pout, mullet and gurnard have all taken pike.

Livebait mounted on double hook trace.

Paternoster ready for casting.

TACTICS AND TECHNIQUES

River piking is often a mobile game, so I prefer a simple tackle arrangement which, with slight alterations, is versatile enough to be used for several presentations of live and dead baits. The first step is to tie a stop knot on the line. Use a simple water knot with Dacron. Next slide on a bead, then the float. Tie the line to the swivel on the trace, and finally add enough swan shot just above the trace to cock the float. With the stop knot set at less than water depth, the rig can be used to trot live and dead baits; sliding it up the line to 24in above water depth permits laying on with a deadbait. Should a float paternoster be necessary, tie a piece of 8lb line between the swivel eye and a leger bomb. For straight legering the float, shot and stop knot are replaced by a bomb.

One drawback is that float paternosters are likely to tangle when the bait twists around trace and line. One solution is to tie in a revolving swivel link, or a three-way swivel; this is an idea I devised for sea fish which is just as good for piking. When you use this, the swivel at the top of the trace should be replaced with a snap link swivel which clips to the bottom of the anti-tangle link. Tangles are very rare with this system.

Trotting is one of the most enjoyable methods and is particularly effective in summer when pike are raring to have a go at any moving target. Start with the bait trotting 9 –12in off the bottom, and adjust the depth if no takes come. Where trees

A lucky catch. The fish snatched a chub bait, and the hook went into the scissors of its jaws.

and obstructions line the bank, the float can be systematically trotted down as far as control permits to cover all the potential pike lies. On clean banks you can follow the float downstream until the bait finds a pike for you.

Stret-pegging works well in streamy water. Set up a float paternoster carrying just enough lead to hold bottom and work it downstream in steps by leaving the bait to rest for a while, then raising the rod tip so that the lead lifts from the bottom. Let out a bit of free line, then stop the float again. Repeat the pattern to send the bait downriver in a straight line from the rod tip.

I notice that many pike anglers habitually cast into midstream and ignore the water under their own bank or tight into the far side. Many of the best pike swims are along the river's edge and that is reason enough to tread quietly and first explore the water under your feet. Pike may congregate in areas of river containing none of the usual clues, and by working the margins and trotting baits downstream you can find the hotspots. Once you have found one, hectic fishing is on the cards.

Float paternostered livebait reigns supreme among the static techniques. One danger of using surface-loving baits like rudd is that pike may engulf the line above

(Opposite) Action is non-stop when you find a shoal of pike.

the trace because the bait has swum upward. The line breaks, and at worst the pike swims away with a mouthful of hooks. It is therefore a wise safeguard to tie in an additional piece of wire slightly longer than the trace and attached above it so that the pike grabs wire not nylon.

Float paternostering is an excellent sit-and-wait method and does offer a good chance of a pike eventually homing in on the bait's erratic struggles, but it does not have to be an immobile system. One of the most productive ways of fishing a river is to creep quietly to the edge of each likely looking spot on the nearside bank and lower the bait directly under the rod tip. Pike rarely resist chomping a bait that appears out of nowhere.

Boat Fishing

Trolling is a highly effective method if you have access to a boat. You can cover virtually every pike haunt on the river. Trolling calls for a meticulous arrangement of tackle, net, etc. in the boat because once a pike is hooked the fisherman must stow the oars, drop anchor, grab the rod and strike all at the same time. It does not help to have bits and pieces of gear lying all

A great introduction for the youngsters.

Weighing a pike in a plastic bag to prevent damaging the fish.

over the boat. Carry the minimum of tackle, keep the boat tidy and work calmly and methodically when the pike takes the bait. It will rarely let go, so there is no need to panic.

A wobbled deadbait is the normal trolling bait, but livebaits do work if you troll very slowly. The bait should trail about 20yd astern and run at about two-thirds of the average water depth. Slowing the boat allows the bait to sink into the deeper holes, and speeding up lifts it over shallow patches. Meanwhile the rod is propped on the stern and the bale arm is open with the line clipped onto the rod handle above the spool. John Roberts line clips are perfect for the job. A pike pulls line out of the clip and takes line freely from the reel.

A small multiplier flicked into free spool, with the ratchet engaged is far superior for trolling. Clips are unnecessary because bites are registered by the ratchet suddenly bursting into life. My Penn 940 Levelmatic incorporates a quiet, sensitive ratchet with just the right amount of tension for trolling. Some reels have ratchets that sound like football rattles; they register the take well but give the fisherman so great a shock that he's likely to jump over the side! Other tackle requirements are the same as those used on the bank, though a very short landing net handle is useful in the restricted space. I use a 30in extra-strong bank stick.

Boats are such excellent sound resonators that tackle banging against the hull will be heard for long distances underwater. Padding the bottom boards with old sacking or carpet serves a dual purpose. It

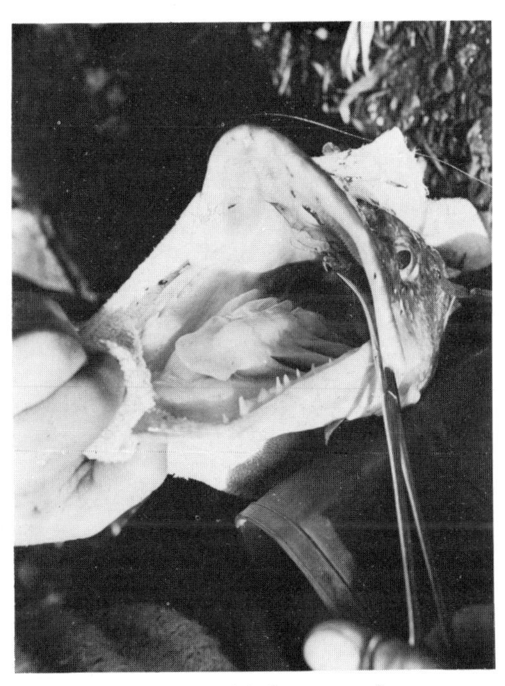

Unhooking is easy with forceps and semi-barbless hooks.

deadens the sounds and acts as a soft surface upon which to lay the pike for unhooking. A responsible pike angler never allows a fish to tear itself to shreds on the bare hull.

Feeding Times

What are the best times of day (or night) to catch river pike? Fish and find out is the only answer, for what applies to one river may be totally wrong on another. Early and late are generally good in summer or winter, and winter time often sees more frequent but shorter feeding spells. Weather conditions have a largely unpredictable effect. A light, warm breeze on a damp, overcast day sets the tingles of anticipation going for me. But one of river piking's attractions is that a fish or two are possible in almost all conditions.

Handling Pike

Perhaps the cold, almost defiant glare of a pike turns some inexperienced anglers' knees to jelly at the mere thought of taking out the hooks. A pike cannot blink with fear, and it does appear to fix you with its stare – unlike most fish its eyes are positioned towards the front of its head. Despite that, unhooking is easy if the captor goes about the job boldly and calmly.

First, turn the pike on to its back. Lay a wet sack or cloth over its body and up to the gill covers. Kneel astride it to prevent it thrashing. Now slide an index finger into the gill arch and lift up the pike's head, whereupon the bottom jaw gapes open. Alternatively wear a thick glove, grip the protruding end of the lower jaw and pull the mouth open. Maintain a firm grip with your knees and finger especially if the pike goes tense, which is a sure preliminary to thrashing. Be the boss – a firm hand will easily restrain your fish.

The only unhooking instrument required is a large pair of forceps which are clamped on the hook shanks. The hooks are pushed free to enable the trace to be withdrawn. If the hooks are set in the throat, insert the forceps through the gill arch. Turn the hooks upside down and they will pop free. Gut-hooked fish should be a rarity for the diligent pike angler, but if it does happen pull gently on the trace until the hooks appear. Then the upside-down treatment works. If it is impossible to reveal the hooks, your only course is to snip the trace as close to the hooks as possible.

A Frosty Day's Piking

One winter's day I peeped through the curtains as the alarm went off to see a snow-like carpet of thick frost, the gaunt branches of the apple tree swinging restlessly to the beginnings of a north-easterly wind. By the time I arrived at the river the wind had increased to a howl, almost cutting off my ears as I emerged from the car. Upstream was a long, wide, very exposed rush-lined straight with good depth and slow flow where I knew lived a lot of pike. Downstream a tree-girded pool contained fewer pike but offered some respite from the icy blast. I reckoned my comfort was more important than abundant pike, so I made tracks in that direction.

I set up two rods, one with floatfished deadbait which I intended to trot down the far bank, the other with float paternostered livebait which would be positioned

(Opposite) Lean and hungry winter pike.

in six feet of water in a slack just downstream on the near bank. For any method of presenting a static bait even when a float is used, I recommend that a butt indicator also is used as a precaution against deep hooking should you not notice the bite on the float.

Drop off indicators are best. The line clips into a brightly coloured polystyrene or table tennis ball which itself is attached to a retaining string anchored to the rear rod-rest. With the line clipped up, the bale arm is opened to allow a fish to pull free line on the take, which pulls line out of the clip so that the indicator drops off. If a pike moves towards the rod as it takes the bait, the indicator slowly falls in response to the slack line.

With the float paternoster in position

Suspend the fish from your index finger. Watch out for the sharp gill rakers though.

and the indicator set, I was attempting to blow some feeling back into my frozen fingers before putting out the trotting rod, when the indicator dropped. Must have set the clip too loose, I thought. The float was nowhere to be seen, and indeed line was spilling steadily from the reel. Still uncertain (the current itself will take line from a spool) I picked up the rod, took the line between finger and thumb and felt for the fish. As the line tightened I felt the unmistakable tap-tug of a pike on the business end. Clicking over the bale arm I wound down until the rod tip bent into the pike, then heaved the rod into its fighting curve.

Striking as such is unnecessary. Just wind in until the rod is well bent against the fish. Even a hefty clout with powerful tackle is ineffective because the pike's vice-like jaws are clamped on to the bait. The power of the strike is thus transmitted into the jaws rather than to the hooks. As you wind down, the pike feels the resistance and opens its mouth to eject the bait. Rod tension then pulls the hooks home.

River pike rarely fail to put up a hard fight even in cold conditions. The one I had hooked had me backwinding the reel furiously and the light 1¾lb rod buckled double as the pike accelerated in an unstoppable rush downstream. But river pike do not run far, so when it stopped I showed the fish who was boss and inched it back by pumping the rod. It surfaced in front of me and looked ready for the net; but I should have known better. The pike surged away again. Trying to stop a sizeable fish in its tracks is just asking for trouble, for pike have incredible speed and power over short distances. In this cold water the fish could not fight for long, though; next time there was no mistake and I pulled it over the rim of the net and on to the bank.

The long, lean bundle of fun I had just caught dragged the scales down to 14¼lb, a fish to be happy about on this stretch of river. I returned her straight away. I fished the paternostered bait in the same slack as before, and trotted a deadbait down the pool's far bank. Forty-five minutes of working the bait into all the lively-looking spots confirmed that a moving bait was out of order in such temperatures. So off with the float and on with a bomb to present the seafood flavour injected roach on the bottom. Half-way through a smoke I heard a click and saw the indicator of the paternoster rod swinging around the back rest. The float slowly submerging toward the middle of the river.

Never wait for second runs before hitting a river pike. Few fish are missed if the tackle is right, and those that are were probably jacks. This time it was a smaller fish of 5–6lb, but welcome anyway. Half an hour later away went the deadbait, making me think I had found a winner by flavouring the bait. Indeed, I believe there really is some scope for experimenting with all sorts of flavours. This pike weighed a shade under 10lb and was hooked nicely in the tip of the lower jaws.

Takes slowed but still came at intervals through the morning on both rods. No pike was larger than the first. The last that took a flavoured bait, a fish of 8lb, proved to be totally blind in both eyes. Healthy pike feed mostly by an amazingly sensitive system of nerve endings on the body which sense water displacement of the prey: they home in, then switch to eyesight for the kill. Yet that blind pike confirms the species' ability to obtain a living by smell alone when it has no alternative.

8 *Zander*

A lot of water has flowed under bridges since that fateful day in 1963 when the Great Ouse River Authority tipped 97 zander fingerlings into the Ouse Relief Channel. Many zander have swum under those same bridges: those 97 fish multiplied rapidly and munched their way through the extensive small fish stocks of the Channel until, rich pickings depleted, they were obliged to migrate towards fresh larders.

Nowadays zander can be found, still munching onward, in river systems all over East Anglia, into the Midlands and beyond – wherever they have been able to penetrate through interconnecting sections of watercourse. Indeed they are found in some rivers that they could never have reached without a little help from an increasing band of zander fans. Doubtless their spread will continue by natural and artificial means until they are distributed through the country.

HABITAT AND BEHAVIOUR

Love them or hate them, zander are here to stay, for no amount of culling will make any serious inroad into the shoals. Higher survival rates in the young is the natural reaction of any group of threatened animals, and zander are no exception. They will do their best to maintain the right balance between their numbers, their habitat and the food stocks available. Probably the best way to cull zander is by thinning out the small fish they feed upon, and to some degree they are doing that themselves. By their own means zander stocks will achieve the same natural balance of population that occurs in Europe where they are a much prized sporting and table fish. Strangely enough, although zanders are prolific breeders they are not successful in every river. The Suffolk Stour is one such, outwardly providing the ideal habitat with plenty of small fish to eat, yet it produces relatively few zander.

Stephen Downes in his book *The New Compleat Angler* tells of Russian research indicating a vulnerability of young zander to the fish louse Argulus, a small jelly-like, kite-shaped parasite which adheres to the host fish and sucks out its juices. These nasty little characters apparently cause little distress to other healthy fish, but the research suggests that four to six lice will kill a year old zander in six hours. I frequently note the presence of Argulus on the roach and bream I hook from the Stour, and they do seem more common than on other rivers. It seems possible that parasitisation of young zander might have prevented overpopulation in the Stour, and perhaps explains the lack of fish in other waterways.

Some enthusiasts believe that the strange, glassy, opalescent eye of the zan-

(Opposite) Magnificent fish like this are still branded as pests by some fishermen.

der indicates that it is predominantly a nocturnal feeder. My own results and those of friends do not altogether support this idea, for in the right conditions we catch more fish during the day. More likely those weird eyes are adapted to be most efficient for hunting when the light reaches a certain level – not complete darkness but perhaps a very subdued light such as the first hour of dawn, at dusk and just after dark. Foul, murky weather would produce similar levels of illumination; and our experiences show that here is the best time of all to catch the species. The main feeding spells of the American walleye, a close relative of zander, have been shown to coincide with similar subdued, but not dark, light levels.

Weather plays a vital role in zander fishing; so much so that now I do not bother to go unless conditions are just right. Anticyclonic patterns with clear skies, bright sun and calm or light winds are worst of all, though the first couple of hours after dawn and the hour before and after dark may produce the odd fish, particularly in summer. Such weather in winter normally means freezing nights, certain to kill any chance of good sport.

Intermittent cloudy and sunny spells

Cold weather zander swim.

with a stiff breeze are better, and zander may feed at intervals throughout the day, takes usually coinciding with cloud cover. The last hour of daylight produces a steady feeding period. Should the skies clear towards evening in winter, the late feeding spell probably will not occur though that time is nearly always reliable in summer and autumn.

Winter or summer, the conditions that fill me with confidence are low pressure periods which bring strong or even gale force southerly or westerly winds with grey clouds scudding overhead often bringing rain. Early and late remain the best times but bites are likely to come throughout the day in these conditions.

Location

Zander are unlikely to be found in numbers in fast-flowing water or the upper reaches of a river. They tend to colonise the middle and lower stretches instead, living in deeper water where the light does not penetrate so far, particularly if the river is coloured. One of the best swims I know of in an otherwise clear river is where the flow is discoloured by discharge from a sewage plant. Snags, overhangs and weedy areas are not the attraction to zander that they are to our other major predators the pike and perch. Zander like open water free from weed beds. However, they do hang around shelves of gullies on the river bed especially where the bottom is reasonably clean sand and gravel. Deep runs alongside marginal belts of rushes are also interesting.

Sometimes on overcast, warm and windy days, zander boil on the surface at dawn and dusk, or they betray their presence by leaving a flat spot in the waves as they swirl just beneath the surface. Zander boils are fairly leisurely, quite unlike the splashy surface strikes of hunting pike. I do not know why zander act like this; the action appears too slow to suggest that they are striking at food fish near the surface, but the activity is a good sign, first because it means you have found the fish, and secondly because a bait cast into the area frequently provokes an immediate take.

Finding the prey fish is as certain a way as any to locate zander. I do not believe that zander are always in the vicinity of their food; rather, they move in when they are hungry. But by fishing amongst the shoals of small fish you can be reasonably sure that before long zander will move into range. Find one zander and you will find others, for they tend to live in packs or groups. Smaller fish up to 2–3lb generally hunt in packs, so when they arrive in your swim sport can be brisk. These little ones are nowhere near as shy as their bigger brothers and sisters. Big fish swim in smaller groups, but they still behave as a pack when they hunt. The very biggest specimens are often loners, or they hunt with one or two more zander of similar size.

What zander do when they are not hunting is anybody's guess. Mine is that they lie inactive close to the bottom in a stretch that offers the depth and flow in which they feel comfortable. No doubt odd fish would be catchable if you found them, but the trouble is having caught one you cannot tell whether it is a resting fish or one member of a hunting pack. Thus, you can waste a lot of time waiting for more fish that never appear.

Bait

Zander prefer fish baits. I have tried most species of freshwater fish as bait, and caught zander on them all. My favourites are dace, chub and roach in that order. Small eel sections are good as well, as are fillets cut from a small zander. I must admit, though, that if I should kill a zander it is much more likely to find its way into my dining room than to be fed back to its cannibalistic parents. They are every bit as tasty as you may have heard, and the flesh is white and firm.

While I have taken zander on deadbaits that have been in and out of the freezer a few times, I have no doubt that fresh baits are much better – preferably they should be caught and killed on the spot. Deadbaits have outfished livebaits by about three zander to one, though in truth I have devoted more time to fishing deads. Based on my experiences alone, the theory is inconclusive. Certainly I can recount days when deadbaits were virtually ignored while livebaits produced plenty of action. Live fish also account for some of the biggest fish of all. Obviously it pays to keep an open mind until you discover what works better on the day. Trial and error is the best system.

Zander prefer quite small baits of about 2–4oz but occasionally they do take bigger ones. The big lone specimens are especially partial to a generous helping. I feel confident with baits about 5in long, anything much larger results in too many fish missed on the strike. If large baits are all that is available, cut them into sections. Head half, tail halves and mid-section cutlets are just as good as whole baits; sometimes they are better probably because the body juices escape into the water more easily to attract the zander. Zander home in quickly to the smell of blood, so always slit open or stab the deadbait before casting out. You may need to puncture the swim bladder anyway or the bait will float. Mind you, an anchored, buoyant bait can be a killer; more about that later.

Everyone knows that bait-sized fish do the disappearing act as soon as you need a few for a zander trip, so it is a good idea to have the freezer permanently stocked with fresh-killed baits which are thus readily available. Frozen baits float, thus a swan shot or two must be added to the trace tight up against the bait. Zander do not mind at all that the bait is frozen rock hard, and sometimes will snatch it as soon as it hits bottom.

Sea fish baits are a total waste of time. If they were the only baits available I would not bother to fish. You may have heard of the odd fish taken on herring, mackerel or sprat but they are the exceptions to the rule. Sprats, being about the right size, are often picked up and spat out straight away. Several years ago a few friends fishing an offshoot of the Suffolk Stour described a series of fast, short takes on sprats intended for pike. On retrieve, they discovered small dual puncture marks on the flanks of the bait. I was in no doubt

Small live and dead fish head the list of zander baits.

about the culprits, and sure enough I caught a number of zander to 7lb plus on my first visit to the spot with small freshwater baits.

The incident made me wonder how many rivers contain an unsuspected population of zander. They do not often show themselves, and spend most of their time in deeper water. River pike fishermen often restrict themselves to sea deadbaits. Putting two and two together, it would not surprise me if zander are more common than generally supposed. Often the first sign of zander is when a fisherman catches one by accident. If you suspect they may be present in your waters but have yet to be hooked, some experimental fishing might pay off.

Drop-back indicators.

TACTICS AND TECHNIQUES

Specialised zander techniques have been slow to develop, most anglers doing well enough with scaled down pike tactics. However, zander do warrant more thought on tackle sensitivity for they can be very cautious feeders, particularly when subjected to heavy fishing pressure. For both livebaits and deadbaits I favour a running leger modified to give maximum sensitivity and to avoid tangles which might prevent line running freely through the swivel when a zander takes. A float paternoster is almost as effective for zander as it is for pike but, although zander like a bait offered this way, a proportion of takes are dropped when the running fish hits the anchor lead.

By using a running paternoster, line can be freely taken through the swivel at the top of the lead link, but in practice the problem is only partially solved because after a short length of line is pulled through the fish meets the resistance of the float. In deeper swims the running paternoster is more viable because more line can be pulled through before the float is felt. Seeing the take as it develops and striking quickly is the best solution.

I have not found trotting particularly good, yet I do know fishermen who have done well. The stretches of river I normally fish are generally too slow for good trotting, and in any case I expect a prowling pack of zander to move into or through my swim sometime during a session, so I prefer to use more or less static baits on leger or paternoster rigs.

The fact that zander do not like sea baits, the need for fresh bait, the value of slitting open the bait to free its juices, and their preference for low-light conditions all back up the idea that much of a zander's scavenging depends on a keen sense of

smell. Always one to experiment, I have therefore legered with a swimfeeder rig filled with an appetising concoction of minced bream stiffened with fish meal – mouth watering stuff. A number of zander have taken freshly killed baits lying along side this 'stink bin' as one friend describes it. However, it is early days and I am not yet convinced that the same fish would not have been caught on a straightforward leger.

A variation of the swimfeeder rig also appears quite successful. Insert a foam tube into an open end feeder then douse the foam with various concentrated flavours like crab, mussel, pilchard, cod liver oil and seafood. Water soluble flavours are best.

Tackle

Many anglers claim that zander do not fight very well, and of course that is true of a fish hooked on heavy pike tackle. On more suitable gear they give a dogged, heavy, thumping resistance, sometimes kiting sideways and with lots of thrashing when they come to the surface. They do not have the same acceleration as river pike though. The power of a zander rod is thus more governed by the weight of the bait and lead it must cast. Even a chub rod will handle zander hooked in open water. A rod of 1¼–1½lb test curve with medium slow action is a good compromise, since it feels nice with a fish on and is powerful enough to lob baits the short distances necessary on the river.

Line strength is matched to the swim and the size of zander expected. I find 8lb test suitable for most situations. More important than precise rod action or line strength is the sensitivity of the terminal set-up, for although the odd unwary fish may fall to crude arrangements most will drop the bait if they feel the slightest resistance from lead, line or bite indicator. Small tandem treble hook rigs are favoured, with the hooks size 12 or 10. Bigger hooks cause dropped takes when the zander feels the hardness of the steel against the softness of the bait. Small hooks take a better hold in the fish's jaws anyway.

I have used wire, nylon and Dacron hook traces often side by side amongst feeding zander. I have no doubt that Dacron produces more confident takes because it is so limp. I have never known a zander to bite through a trace. They do not have the same cutting teeth as pike; rather, the teeth are wider spaced with prominent canines towards the front of the jaws for stabbing and gripping the prey. But wherever pike are likely to be hooked by accident (and realistically that probably means most places) it is irresponsible to use Dacron or monofilament. The result might well be a bitten-through trace and a poor old pike with a mouthful of trebles that could kill him. In those circumstances, use a light wire trace even if it does cost you a few zander.

Handling and Unhooking

Handle your zander with care, for they are very susceptible to damage. Unhooking can be done in the same manner as for pike. You will find that a zander's jaws are tremendously strong and need a very firm hand. The tandem treble rig enables an instant strike so hooks should be in the front of the jaws.

(Opposite) Watch your fingers. Zander have ferociously powerful jaws.

Dorsal fin spines and sharp gill covers can draw blood if you are careless. The best way to hold a zander is with the hand under the middle of its belly. The fish is rough to the touch and not the least slippery. A zander held this way tends to stiffen and stays immobile except for a few wags of its tail. I see no reason to retain zander in nets except for a short time while cameras are prepared for a big fish. Zander are not the tough customers they appear to be – even if you must keep them, use a carp sack which is much kinder than a net.

A Zander Session

I fish for zander in winter more than summer, being occupied with other species in the warmer months. The awaited 'right' conditions were a long time coming last winter but mid January at last saw the arrival of a big depression bringing wild force 8 south-westerlies and squally downpours of rain that sent ordinary mortals scurrying for shelter. It was the second day of the depression when I made it to the river by which time the rain had added flow and colour – perfect conditions.

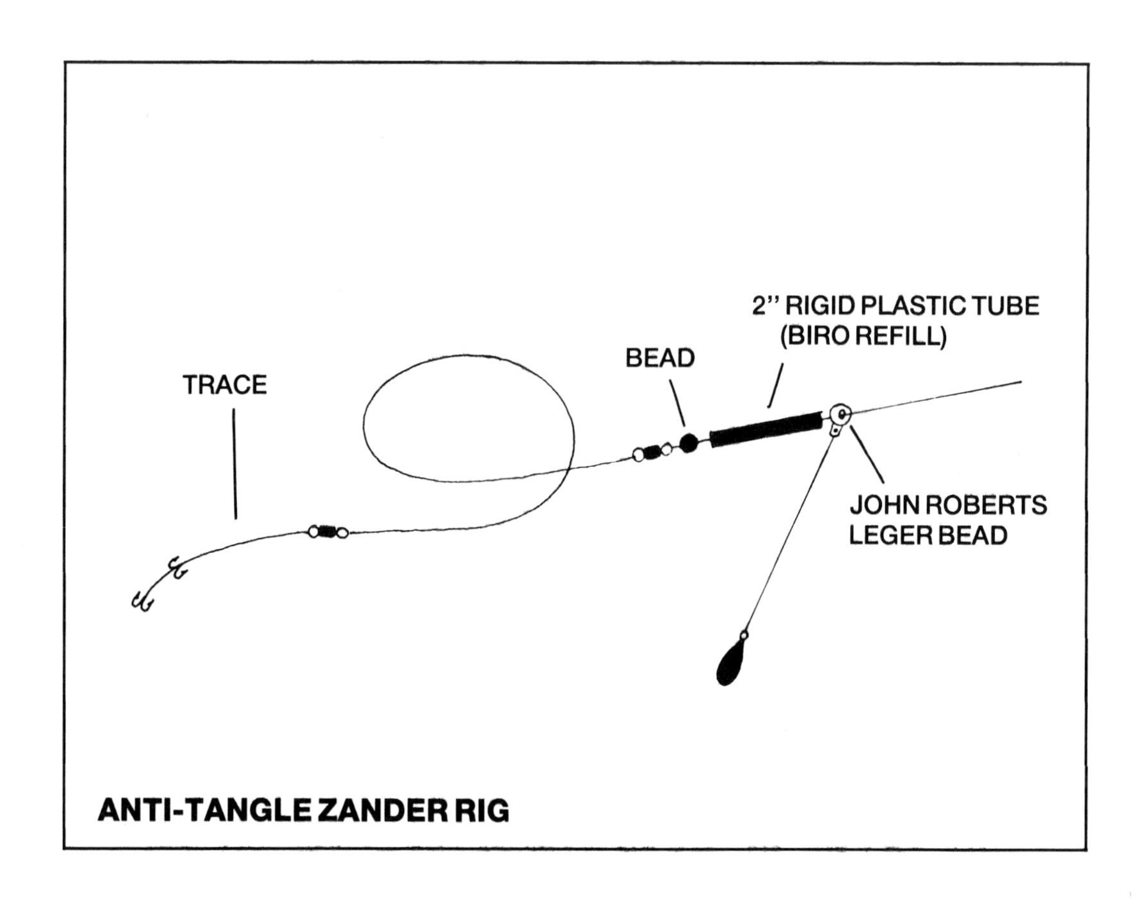

ANTI-TANGLE ZANDER RIG

Opalescent eye, small jaws and dog teeth are characteristic of zander.

I set up two rods on a wide, deep bend. One with a leger rig to fish a static dead roach on the bottom at mid-river, the other with float paternoster to offer a deadbait just off the bottom in a gully close to my bank. I did not anticipate pike in the coloured river. They feed little in these conditions, so I considered it safe to use a Dacron trace on both rods.

I was soon in action. The drop-off indicator I use for piking fell from the line on the leger rod and I struck into a medium sized zander that subsequently weighed in at 5¾lb, nicely hooked in the front of the jaws. I am always glad that I nip the barbs off the hooks not holding the bait – the trebles come free so much more easily and do little damage.

Predictably, it was all action for the first two hours with takes on both rods, all from fish in the same bracket as the first – not big but fun. Just as predictably, takes became more cautious as fish picked up the bait, pulled off an inch or two of line, then felt the resistance of the indicator and dropped the deadbait.

On some rivers virtually every bite is a belter with line fairly hissing from the spool. But on others those shy little pulls and tugs at the bait are just normal zander behaviour. There are several ways to remedy the problem. One is to allow the indicator to hang well below the reel. At the first sign of a bite, unhook the line before it tightens, then feed slack line to the fish which thus runs more confidently with the bait. A second way is to hover over the rod, bale arm closed, and strike at the first sign of life. With a small bait and tandem trebles the fish is usually hooked despite the tiny bite.

If resistance has already caused the bait to be dropped, give the line a long, hard pull so that the bait jerks along the bottom. Zander cannot resist that and usually have another go. An excellent way to induce confident takes is to dispense with indicators altogether. The bait is either freelined with no lead at all or is presented on a leger rig. After casting, twitch the bait – live or dead – back along the bottom. Give a short pull, let the bait pause, then twitch it again, and so on. The rod is held throughout, pointed at the bait, and a spare loop of line is held ready to be quickly released when a take occurs.

At times a buoyant deadbait twitched along the bottom on a leger rig proves deadly. Tugging and pausing imparts a see-saw motion which encourages zander to attack. The bait is made buoyant by leaving the swim bladder intact, or if it still persists in sinking by pushing a chunk of polystyrene foam into its mouth. Frozen baits will float until they thaw – or until a zander nabs them.

9 *Tackle and equipment*

Kitting yourself out with the right tackle for river fishing will not ensure instant success. What you do with your tackle is infinitely more important than which particular items you choose. For the most part, selection is an individual affair anyway, and you can do no better than opt for good quality along with the performance characteristics you personally prefer.

Specific descriptions and suggestions appear throughout the book, thus there is no need to repeat myself here. To some extent the rods you choose must fall in line with the design and feel you like, how much you wish to spend, and of course with the way you approach the sport. The same philosophy applies equally to reels, and indeed to every piece of equipment you buy. If there is an overall recommendation, it is to look for quality, for it is an inescapable fact of life that a fair proportion of the tackle sold for coarse fishing is poorly designed and badly built. Short life, low performance and unreliability are inevitably followed by increasing disappointment, frustration and sometimes pure rage. Stick to well-made tackle of respected brand names, and if necessary build up your outfit gradually rather than waste money by starting with a complete set of inferior equipment.

LINES

I try all the new lines as they become available, and always go back to Maxima. Other fishermen swear by Sylcast, Bayer Perlon and other premium brands. It really boils down to choosing the balance of cost, performance and quality that you like. Perhaps more important than brand is the need to change lines regularly, which is easier and cheaper if you buy bulk spools. My lines are replaced at least three times every season, and I have little sympathy for anglers who use the same nylon for ages then whinge when they lose a big fish.

NETS

For some years I have grown increasingly unhappy about using keepnets. Even soft, knitted meshes damage fish because they rub off slime and scales. Perch, zander and barbel are trapped by their spiny fins and gill covers. Lately I have used a modified nylon carp sack with a large ring and bank-stick fitting around the opening. The sack is held open just like a regular keepnet but there is a world of difference in the way it treats the fish. They remain in perfect condition and I never find loose scales in the bottom of the sack.

I doubt if I shall use a traditional keepnet again, and I look forward to the day when a manufacturer introduces a 'proper' keepnet built on the sack principle with long tubular body, full set of supporting rings and an opening bottom held shut with a toggle and draw cord. By slackening the cord you could release fish from the bottom of the net, a much neater and kinder operation than normal.

I have known fishermen buy landing nets as a symbol of prowess: big net, big white hunter! It is true that a capacious

Several rods are necessary for all-round river work. However, precise design is less important than personal preference and good quality.

net lands small fish as well as big ones but even so it is illogical to encumber yourself with too large a model for all-round fishing. Mostly I use three different nets. The smallest, used for roach, dace, etc., is a 15in diameter round frame with shallow, knitted mesh. The largest is a triangular framed pike model with 42in arms, 30in deep and flat-bottomed netting. The flat bottom is important because if you use the tapered version on pike, they roll themselves up into a horrible tangle of mesh, fish and treble hooks. The ideal net for pike also has dual meshing – large mesh on the sides to minimise waterlogging, and small mesh stitched into the base to support the fish.

For chub, barbel and zander I use a 24in diameter round frame net which despite being light is big enough to cope if I chance upon a bigger species. Its frame carries a very deep 40in mesh for a very good reason: a lot of my chub fishing is the roving kind, and because I dislike returning some species straight away, chub included, I retain them in the landing net for the short period I am working their swim. The net being so deep, I can still land a fish without losing three or four already inside.

Small mesh is kinder, but a large waterlogged net becomes so heavy that it cannot be used in fast water unless you have arms like a gorilla's. My barbel net therefore uses large mesh netting which allows the current to flow through rather than hit what amounts to a solid wall of small meshes.

ACCESSORIES

One of my favourite occupations is poking about in my friends' tackle boxes to find out what they use. Since it is not unusual to have my own tackle rooted through, I conclude that most fishermen are equally fascinated by bits and pieces of equipment.

Tupperware are probably unaware of it, but their partitioned box about 12in by 8in with removable inner tray is just about perfect for storing sundry fishing accessories. In mine I store boxes of shot ranging from No.4 to SSG, a bread punch with three interchangeable metal punches – small for dace, medium for roach and very large, about 1in diameter, for chub. There is also a tape measure, screw top containers for float caps, swivels, beads, etc., a spool of ½lb nylon for tying hair rigs, bombs up to 1oz, and a few scraps of expanded polystyrene foam for making buoyant rigs. Individual tiny balls picked out of the foam and slid on to the hook make an effective and different method of presenting maggots, casters and red worms.

The box also holds link leger rigs, a tube of superglue, a pair of nail clippers for trimming knots, a tub containing leger

Flat bottomed landing net.

stops and another filled with Drennan metal rings which I use for paternoster rigs. There are a few pieces of silicone rubber tube which stiffens link legers and prevents tangling with the main line. What else? Stray floats, Drennan hook disgorgers small and large, a hypodermic syringe for blowing air into lobworms and deadbaits and for squirting in flavours, a thermometer, a hook sharpening stone and a pencil. All of them fit into that one small Tupperware box.

Another hinged plastic box holds packets of Partridge Specialist and Kamatsu eyed hooks in sizes from 18 to 2. I prefer eyed hooks to spade ends and I never use hooks ready whipped to nylon – if a knot fails I want it to be my own fault.

Sometimes you can scrounge from an art shop tubular plastic containers that once held paintbrushes. Being rigid they make perfect float boxes. One should hold most of the floats a river fisherman requires: a few wire stemmed stick floats, Avons and peacock stem wagglers in a range of sizes appropriate to waters and tactics.

BAGS AND SEATS

Anglers who have yet to discover the considerable advantages of a hiker's rucksack are in for a pleasant surprise. I use a Karrimor Tote-Em Senior, a framed sack with many pockets that swallow flasks, food, spare clothing and anything else I might need, plus tackle of course. Make sure you buy a rucksack with a waistband that buckles down tightly to spread the load over your hips rather than just on the shoulders. It is so comfortable that you will forget it is on your back, and those distant and unfished swims become a more viable proposition than they are if you are loaded down with a traditional box.

A chair with adjustable legs is a boon for river fishing, for more often than not you will be fishing on awkwardly sloping banks. The Ever Level available from good tackle shops is not cheap but does enable you to fish almost any swim in comfort. It is also the right height – perhaps I'm getting old but I do have a devil of a job getting out of a low chair in a hurry. Avoid chairs with arms. They prevent a sideways strike, which is what you do most of the time on rivers.

For short fishing sessions I leave the chair in my van and carry an inflatable cushion instead. It fits into my pocket and takes only a puff of air to inflate. If I need to take the chair, it is strapped to the rucksack along with my rod rests thus leaving both hands free to carry rods, net handle and perhaps a groundbait bucket.

TACKLE STRATEGY

By watching weather and river conditions you can predetermine which species to go for, so there is no need to take all your tackle on every trip. Nowadays I never carry more than two rods: a pair of pike or zander rods or a light leger rod and a 13ft trotter for other species if I need a more flexible approach with a wide variety of styles.

My two-sectioned rods are always made up beforehand because then I can get down to the important business of catching fish without losing time on the bank. As a matter of fact my much-used chub rods are left permanently assembled unless I need to change lines or make a repair. Do not try that with three-piece rods though. The mess you get into is not worthwhile.

Two piece rods can be held together with elastic bands top and bottom, and do not need a rod bag. I have not used a holdall for many years; instead I carry rods and net handle (and umbrella if neces-

A strong, versatile seat is a worthwhile investment.

sary) by bundling them together with Velcro straps. However, it seems to me that today's roll-up holdalls which accept made up rods might be worth a second look. The Happy Hooker version looks handy.

NIGHT FISHING

Night fishing on rivers is not always the way towards bigger and better catches. On the other hand I can think of many chub, roach and bream swims that come alive after dark, especially with the bigger specimens. Personally I regard night fishing with a few friends along some quiet, remote river one of the most enjoyable aspects of the sport. Tactics are no more complicated than they are in daylight provided you are reasonably familiar with the swim or stretch of river. Unknown spots have a habit of throwing up problems like bad snags. Trees that sit tight all day seem to creep up and grab your tackle when you cast at night.

Knowing the lie of the land helps avoid most mishaps, and there should be no need to use a torch except to tie hooks or sort out tangles. A friend who watches for bites by illuminating his rod with a torch once called me over to see a group of chub that were gathered where the beam hit the water. Obviously the light had attracted them. The point to remember is that a stationary beam does not scare fish, but they will not stand for lights being switched on and off or being flashed about. Moreover, the less you use artificial illumination, the better adjusted to the dark your eyes become; indeed, the less you use a torch, the less you need it anyway.

Betalights are superb night fishing aids. Leger rods need a moderately powerful betalight fixed on the tip at right angles to the blank. Mine are 300 microlamberts output and whipped permanently to the tip. As good as quivertips are for bite detection, I never use them after dark because they are prone to line tangling, a problem considerably aggravated by the addition of a betalight tube.

Betalights can play tricks with your eyes. You are certain the tip is moving but it is actually an optical illusion. The best way is to avoid staring directly at the pinpoint of light. Instead, crook the line around your finger and feel for the bite as well; when the betalight moves you will then be left in no doubt.

Night trotting is effective when you use a float capped by a powerful 500 microlambert betalight. Bites are unmistakable because one moment the bright blob rides away in the darkness, the next it has disappeared. The float is a joy to use once the fish is hooked; it throbs and dances in the blackness indicating where the fish is and what it is doing. These powerful lights are expensive. Take the precaution of stepping up the main line's breaking strain and using a lighter hook length below the float so that in the event of a snap you do not lose the float.

Although I hate unnecessary gimmicks, I am interested in a new gadget from Sundridge Tackle called the Fish Finder. It is a small tube with betalight enclosed and is attached to the line when you are legering. It indicates which way a fish is heading at short range, and makes a positive target to grab when you wind in to rebait. The gadget is so designed that the light drops into a black tube as soon as the leger sinks, so presumably it does not show up underwater. The tube automatically inverts during retrieve, sliding the betalight into the transparent end of its tube.

WINTER CLOTHING

Fishing can be a cold business. Midwinter conditions on the river, night-time especially, can freeze your landing net to the bank, weld line to rod rings and turn fingers and toes to ice. A dab of glycerine on the rings helps prevent line freezing to them, and you can always dunk the net into the river to thaw. But what of the fisherman himself? Nobody enjoys fishing chilled to the bone.

Good clothing shrugs off all but the most severe conditions. Start with a string vest followed by a long-sleeved thermal vest, then a moleskin shirt and two loose-fitting wool sweaters. On top of all that go a sleeveless insulated waistcoat and warm scarf. Dressing the lower half begins with a pair of thick woollen socks, fleecy-lined or thermal long pants, a pair of thick trousers and then waxed cotton overtrousers. Finally, pull on a lightweight, windproof coat with a sensibly large hood. Cold feet are a thing of the past since the arrival of thermal lined Arctic boots. Mittens and warm hat take care of the other extremities.

Dressed thus you will resemble a cross between an Abominable Snowman and a refugee from Bangladesh, but you will stay warm enough to enjoy your fishing, and will still be catching fish when the other anglers are huddled around the fire.